MW01172158

God
Send Me A'
Good Woman

Rae Zellous

Chapter 1

LET'S BEGIN WITH HEARTBREAK

I believed that I had found her, had finally found true love. I was ready to commit, close the deal, turn my player's card in. Something told me that the woman that slept beside me day after day, night after night, month after month, year after year, was the "one." Never did I think hour by hour, minute by minute, second after second, I would grow to hate this woman. A woman of independence, of strength, of intelligence, of power, of beauty. Was so scorned, was full of malignity, so scarred, and was so full of hurt herself that she would hurt and be so harmful to what she had uncaged from deep inside of me, my love.

She had unlocked my vascular organ from its depth of deep, blinding shade and brought it in to a radiance of light where she could heal it, nurture it back to health and fill it back up with compassion, emotional affection, our love, or so I believed. But how could she be selfish but so giving, nonchalant but thoughtful, beautiful but yet, so damn ugly inside. She blamed me. How could she?! How dare she?!

A man of independence, of strength, of intelligence, of power, of knowledge. I had so much to give, but it still wasn't enough. I was fatigued and exhausted, constantly. Mentally drained, constantly. I expected her to be there physically. I needed her to provide a stress-free home. Instead, she worked as hard as I did and she was never home. She was never home, but neither was I. She was a mirroring-image of me.

Ambition had gotten the best of us, had moved us in separate directions making us highly successful on our own, but a consolidated failure, together.

Roses bought, crumbled and withered, from lack of sunlight and water. The wine remained chilled, dinner was never cooked, jewelry and designer business-wear were bought for the office. Our jobs were our spouses being served court orders of separation. And there I was desperately waiting for a switch to click and turn on. I was back in the dark, back where I began, in torturing loneliness.

What I thought to be perfect had become a bullet, metaphorically speaking. A bullet that killed all I had left inside of me to give, to share. And *my wife's* finger had

4

pulled the trigger, standing opposite of me with the smoking gun in her hand. She had murdered love, trust, and my sex-drive with one shot, "POW!" I was dead, but still functioning. Somewhat like some type of broken-hearted zombie. I was the walking dead. Of course I was. She was gone, and how can a man live without his heart?

Now here I was thinking of my wife, while feasting on another woman's succulent breast. Drooling, dribble trickled from my stiff-tongue flickering feverishly back-and-forth across her erect nipple. I fondled the other, looking up at her, while I worked that damn nipple. Her head tossed around, her neck was arched back, "Aaagh...Mm hm," translation, she wanted to cum.

I pulled my hand from her shaved sex-spot, and with my middle finger I smeared her love juices over her right papilla, gathered her breasts together, and ran my mouth across both of them.

Her legs parted further and further apart, my pussy-beater throbbed, fiending to enter her. Hell, she begged me to, but I made her wait.

Listening to her beg more and more, I finally grabbed her by her legs, and flipped her over on all fours, "Spread ya ass cheeks," I demanded. Rubbing my manhood up and down her wet holes, I entered the lower, "Aagh, baby," I groaned out.

Twenty minutes later, I watched her nude ass sway up and down, as her beautiful body, fully exposed, walked to her bathroom. Hearing the bathroom water running, I readied myself for the hot soapy rag she would bring in to wipe me off with. Afterwards, I sat at the edge of her bed, after gathering my expensive church clothes mixed with hers from off of the carpeted floor.

"What am I doin' here," I asked myself, putting on my socks, boxers, and suit. "WHAT AM I DOIN' HERE?!" The voice inside of me asked again as I put my tie in my suit-jacket pocket.

Clarissa Goodman, the lead singer of the church choir, and I, Keelan Rockmon, were members of Bethlehem Church. A church where I had met many of my female companions. Since my divorce, I had made my way into many of the female attendees' bedrooms, but for some reason, this time I felt different. Guilt started setting in after we had sex. This time was different from the last, different from the rest. Was it the Pastor's message?

The Pastor preached 1 Timothy 2:8. "So I want men everywhere to pray with holy hands lifted up to God, free from sin and anger and resentment," he read from scripture.

God's Word echoed louder-and-louder in my head, but the more I thought, the more Clarissa touched me. When I flinched she realized how much she was starting to annoy me and backed off.

"I gotta get outta here," my insides cried out. I needed to leave and clear my conscience.

Standing, I looked down at my suit, it made me think of the tuxedo I wore to my wedding, even though it looked nothing like it. Oh yeah, by the way, I'm divorced. I forgot to mention it...

I know, calm down, we'll get into that in a second.

Anyway, like I was saying, the sex was good, but the Pastor's message was better.

"Are you gon' call me later?" Clarissa asked.

It was routine, "Yeah," I said, walking towards the front door.

Truth is, we didn't care about each other. Standing in the opened doorway, we pecked each other on the lips and hugged. Humph, she didn't care if I called or not, and to be honest, I wouldn't. Our thing was a sex thing. My dick just gave us more to repent about.

God Send Me A Good Woman

Outside of Clarissa's, I sat in my Land Rover and pounded my fist against the steering wheel with tears in my eyes. I hated failure, and I had failed. Failed at marriage, and according to the Pastor, I was failing at being obedient to God. I had so much to repent for, and there I was compelled to pray, "God, send me ah good woman." Raising my voice as it cracked from the pain I felt, I cried out again, "GOD, SEND ME AH GOOD WOMAN!" I prayed and prayed until my phone rung.

Looking at my phone, I wished it was God answering my call, but it wasn't, it was my cousin, "Hey, cuz...Snst..." There was a moment of silence on the phone-line. "Nigga, is you cryin'?"

"Hmph, nah...Why you say that?" I wiped tears from my eyes. "Why would I be cryin'?"

"Ah, maybe 'cause ya ass is still in love with Payton, and you want her back so bad, ha ha ha..."

"Ha ha ha, fuck you, cuz."

"Look, I just got to the shop. You comin' to getcha hair cut or what? I'm only here 'cause of ya ass. So getcha ass over here."

"Ha, I'm on my way."

"How long?"

8

"I'm on my way. Give me like ten," I said to my cousin.

He hung up without saying another word. He left me looking at my phone, saying, "Hello...Hello," and shaking my head.

My cousin, Larry Young, and I, grew up together. He knew me very well. He was a few years older, and a lot wiser then I was. Well, at least, in the woman department. But even he had woman problems at times. He's been kicked out of his house and slept in my guest room on several occasions. It was crazy that he knew what I was going through about "her." When I say "her," I mean my wife, ugh, my ex-wife...Payton.

Payton Crawford-Rockmon was raised in South Philadelphia, but had spent most of her summers in Pittsburgh, Pennsylvania growing up as a kid. Her parents had gotten divorced when she was nine-years-old. Her father had taken a job with the Pittsburgh Corridor, and had moved to Pittsburgh after the divorce. He's been working there ever since. Payton, graduated from Pitt University where I had met her. Now, as a journalist herself, working for BNN, Black National News, she covered the news all over the world. I couldn't turn on the TV without getting a glimpse of her. She was all over the news, even at my job where I work for her father at the Courier. Mr. Crawford was very understanding of our divorce. He had gone through a similar separation with her mother.

Pulling up at Oscar's Barbershop, I pulled close to the curb, and shifted the gear into park. I jumped out and pushed a button on my keychain to lock the doors of my Land Rover, and headed inside of Oscar's, my cousin Larry's barbershop. Inside, Marsha Ambrosius's, *Cheats On You*, played. "I hope she cheats on you, with a basketball player," she sung. She was one of my favorite artist, but Jill Scott was my all-time favorite. Marsha's song was being used as a tool of ridicule towards me.

When I walked into the barbershop, three grown-ass men burst out in laughter like three six-year olds, holding their stomachs, pointing at me.

"Was mama's we-wool bay-be cryyy'in?" One of the jokers said and more laughter followed.

"What?!" I was puzzled, then it hit me. I had walked in the barbershop bobbing my head to Marsha's vengeful tune, then I stopped bobbing my head, and caught the lyrics. "FUCK Y'ALL!" I said with my nostrils flaring.

Taking off my coat, I hung it up, and took a seat in my cousin's chair. Shaking my head, I gritted at two of the laughing hyenas. Then I turned to see if my cousin was laughing, he was. He spun away from facing me, acting like he was tending to his clippers, but his jerking shoulders told me he was laughing too.

"Whoa," I released air from my mouth and closed my eyes. "Come on, cut my fuckin' hair, so I can get outta here man."

"Don't be mad at us 'cause ya wife is cheating on you with ah bas-ket-ball play-ah, cuz," my cousin said putting a thin, white neck-strip around my neck. He had played the song purposely to mess with me.

Payton's new boyfriend, Jahlil, was a NBA player that played for the Sixers. The two of them had been plastered all over the tabloid magazines and Entertainment News. How could I forget, they definitely weren't going to let me.

"Oh, fuck!"

The Barber's cape flew over my head, and my cousin wrapped it around my neck, and tightly snapped it fastened.

"Hand me the remote, cuz," I told my cousin, Larry. He handed it to me, and I pushed next on the song that belittled me. The next song played was *Something Just Ain't Right* by Keith Sweat.

The small group of family and friends hysterically laughed.

I sat up, looked sideways up in the air, and shook my head, angered. Evidently this was a slow jam tape put together just to mess with me. I hit next again, *Alone Together* by Marsha began to play and their laughter continued.

The song was about being alone and lonely, but also about not wanting to be alone and being alone with someone you could live the rest of your life with stranded on a remote Island. An island of sunshine, happiness, repetitious harmonic bliss, good nature, tolerance, consideration, benevolence, kindness, decency, merriment, exhilaration, jollity, glee, and all the other fuckin' stuff that means "Happy." Shit! What's wrong with being alone with the person that makes you happy?

Anyway, the song was too good to skip. The louder my friends laughed, the louder I raised the volume. Marsha's angelic voice gave me tranquility. My crew was too busy to recognize that Marsha had bought me to tears. I hurried and wiped the tear that fell from the corner of my eye. I was that hurt inside, and her voice had gotten to the depth of my soul, and began to sing sweet serenades of chivalry to my malfunctioning heart. I closed my eyes as if

God was putting me into a deep sleep like he did with Adam. It was like he was taking out my rib, and creating someone else for me to love. "Bone of my bone, flesh of my flesh." Then my cousin Larry snatched the remote from my hand, bringing me out of my soporific love trance. "What the fuck, cuz?!"

"Boy, turn this shit down. I'm try'na cut hair, not get arrested."

"My fault, cuz. I was just gon' for ah second on some Adam and Eve stuff," I told my cousin.

"What?!" He asked.

I looked back at him. His face showed his confusion.

"That was ah good message the Pastor preached," my cousin said placing his buzzing clippers to the side of my head.

"Yes, it was," I replied, closing my eyes trying to get back that loving feeling Marsha gave me. Then there she was, Payton, in a damn lyric. The lyric reminded me of our wedding.

"When you the desert sand, I'll be the water," Marsha sung.

Missing You by Case was me and Payton's favorite song, and in that song, Case sings, "...I'm the desert without the sand." I know the lyrics didn't mean the same thing but desert and sand in both songs made me think of my ex-wife.

"Yo Kee, did you say Adam and Eve?" Our friend, Gabrielle "Cabby" George, asked. Him and our other friend, Shane Townes, always joined us at the barbershop on Sunday's. We were all members of Bethlehem Church.

Cabby, actually drove a cab, and Shane was bootlegger. He kept the latest CDs and DVDs. He often complained about how slow business was, but drove a Cadillac, owned his own house and was the only one married out of us. Go figure.

"Okay, Cabby, what about Adam and Eve?" I asked.

Cabby, always had some kind of love theory about the interactions of couples in the Bible.

"Naw, it ain't just them, though, Kee. I was reading the Bible the other day, and I got deep in the word. I was like, man, this is crazy. Cause God was just openin' up stuff to me. Stuff I know he ain't given to nobody else. That's how I know he loves me, man, cause he don't drop it on y'all

like that. He gives it to me to give to ya'll, and I'ma hav'tah start given it to the pastor!"

"Oh, no, buddy. You just need to keep ya thoughts in the shop, or at least, let us check it out first." My cousin, Larry, told Cabby.

"Hell, yeah, Cab," I said.

Shane pulled out his Galaxy, "I gotta record this," he said, pushing record on his phone.

"Okay, look, God said, let us make human beings in our image to be like us. And male and female, he created them..."

"Mm hm," I expressed my approval, holding my dreads up as my cousin shaped the back of head up.

"Neither man nor' woman is made more in the image of God more than the other. God formed man from the dust of the ground. He breathed the breath of life into man's nostrils, and man became a living person. Then God gave his commandments of dos and don'ts to man, and told him what would kill him. The only thing that would make him fall out wit' him, you know..."

"This boy's trippin'," Shane said.

"Naw, listen. Then God made woman, but when he made woman, he dug inside of man, and pulled a part of man out, and he closed him up. God was doin' surgery on ah brotha. He had ah brotha under anesthetic and all that, you know."

15

"Oh, lawd," I said as my cousin shaped my beard up.

"Look, while man was in ah deep sleep, God, developed woman. That's why we can't figure 'em out, man! That's why we don't know how they function and stuff! And just like ah man, when we see ah bad female, we lose it. We don't think about nothin', but hittin' that. We don't think about no kinda details. Like when we be watchin' ah woman, but we don't realize that our woman is watchin' us watch that female. And, you know, like, we don't be asking is this woman and me compatible, or is this woman gon' be trouble for us."

"Okay, Cab'. I hear you," Shane said getting a better recording position on Cabby.

"Cause, like, God, brought woman to man, and instead of man getting to know woman before he married her, he just started spittin' game, droppin' poetry on her. He was like, *this one is*

bone from my bone, and flesh from my flesh! Wit' an exclamation point. Then he was like, *she will be called woman, because she was taken from, man.* So look, that's where we get our game. Adam was spittin' game from the door. That's why Satan was playah hatin' on him. Plus, he was mad cause God was messin' wit' him like that. He was his son, Jesus', new man's..."

"Ha, ha, ha," we all laughed, but Cabby had our attention. We all was listening. What he was saying was interesting. He had ah way of puttin' ah hood-spin on the Bible.

"But yo though, listen. Me, y'all know me, and how deep in the word I can get. I'm reading the word like, hol' up! How the hell did Adam know that God made woman from his rib? What? Did he wake up like, *'Yo! God, why you knock me out?'* I'm feelin' ah lil groggy around this joint..."

"Ha, ha, ha!" Cabby had us dying. My cousin, Larry, had to stop trimming my beard to get a good laugh.

"Listen, Adam's naked ass probably was like, *'Why my side hurt. Oh, God, wassup?! Where this damn scar come from?'*

We all were in tears, laughing as Cabby continued.

"*'God, you put me to sleep, and I'm hurtin', sore, tore, and sown up. What's up?'* Then Jesus, probably pulled back some branches in the garden and he showed him woman. And Adam, probably was like, *'Oooh...Yo, who dat?'* And Jesus was like, *'Dat's what I was try'na tell you, my Father, made you ah woman. He took out one of ya ribs to do it, but me and my spiritual brothas, the angel's, and all dem, watched 'im. He put some'in' nice together fo' you'.*"

We all were still laughing. I fell out of my chair listening to Cabby's Adam and Eve scenario.

17

"Seeing how bad woman was he was ready to marry her off the dribble. He had been on Earth, tending to all of God's business, but he started trippin' cause he was lonely. That's why God said, *'It's not good for the man to be alone. I will make him a helper'.* Not only did God give man a woman. He gave his man Adam, Gold, Onyx, Gush, and Tigris. He put him in charge of everything. And after God "personally," married Adam and Eve, he said to Adam, *'Now go do you, go multiply...'*"

"Oh, that's how he told Adam?" I asked holding my stomach from laughter.

"Yeah, see Adam was so hyped-up when he seen Eve, he wanted to go straight to the alter. Instead of Adam asking for God's knowledge of the situation, he took on woman by himself. He just started spitting game off the rip. I would've be like, 'Look Father, you the all-knowing, what's up wit' her? Is she gon' do me right, or is she gon' play me?' See, if he would've asked God about Eve before he married her, God would've told him, *'Look Adam, Eve is bad, and all that, but ah...I'ma make you another woman...'*"

"Aw, I had enough." My cousin had finished shaping me up, and I was ready to go. I know Cabby could go on and on, so I shook my homies hands, and was out.

"Hol' up Kee, you outta all people need to hear why woman act so crazy when another man comes along. You know, like when Satan comes in to play."

"Shane is recording everything you're saying, I'll check it out later. I'm out."

Chapter 2

A REFLECTION OF SELF

It was the second of December, and a light snow had covered my Land Rover. Getting inside of my SUV, I started the engine, blew into my gathered hands, and rubbed them together to keep them warm. I had left my phone in my truck, lightly hitting the on/off button on the side of it to make its screen light up. I had two missed calls and six messages including a Facebook Messenger alert. Looking in my side mirror, I seen a car approaching to pass me by. I waited until it did, and pulled away from the curb into traffic. Throwing my phone back into the passenger's seat, I thought about what Cabby was saying, and chuckled.

Halfway towards Downtown Pittsburgh, I had my foot on my brake at a stoplight. Checking my Horoscope, I surfed the Internet on my smartphone. When 2 Thessalonians 3:5 came to mind, *'Now may the Lord direct your hearts into the love of God and into the patience of Christ.'* It was as if God was trying to tell me to allow him

20

to direct my heart into love and to be patient. "Okay, let's see what my Horoscope says," I voiced driving down Penn Avenue, thumbing '12.22-01.19, Capricorn:

'Who says gold stars are only for grade schoolers? On the 20th, glittering praise from higher ups may cement your celestial status. Make sure your online presence is up to snuff when a second wave of attention hits you on the 25th. You need: To balance your optimism with realism.'

"Hm, nothing! I don't know why I mess with that stuff," I remarked, sitting my phone on my lap, riding to my Penn Avenue Apartment.

I stayed at the Lando Lofts, Downtown. My Loft was right above the Robert Clemente Bridge, across from Pittsburgh's PNC Park where the Pirates played. With a top floor view, I could watch the game from there. On hot summer days, I sat on the balcony and thought, looking out at the panoramic view of lights and bridges. Easily making it down Penn Avenue, I signaled to pull into my parking garage when I saw a familiar face. It was Wyoni Sumpter, a friend of mine. She was motioning her hands as if to say something to me.

"Wy', what you doin'?" I rolled down my window and asked.

"Larry told me you were headed home, so I came down to see you. Why ain't you answer your phone?" She asked looking both ways at the traffic then she crossed the street to get in my truck.

"I was going to call you once I got in the house," I lied.

"Don't park, let me treat you to something to eat. Where you wanna go, Olive Garden, Ruth Chris...?"

"How 'bout Primanti Brother's? I don't have a lot of time. I have some writing to do."

"Okay, we can do that...What you writing?" She asked once she got in the car and put on her seat belt.

"Something on mental health for the Corridor."

"Hm, I can't wait to read it."

My friend, Wyoni Sumpter, is a proud mother of a son that attends college. When I met her she was a teen mom that was striving to raise her son without flaw as my mother did, raising me as a single parent. Now, Wyoni, was the president and CEO of the Hope House Association, and bestselling author of, *Look Back to Give Back*, a book on philanthropy. Her blog and lucrative endorsements has caused a social impact. Her generosity reached beyond the hood to youth services all over the world. She was credited for making strong-minded, young adults out of juvenile delinquents plagued by inadequacies. A statuesque red bone with perks. Her body is voluptuous and full-figured. She's striking and well-proportioned. Her straight, white teeth displayed a radiant smile. Her hair is somewhat curly at the ends, and falls to her shoulders, onto her large breast.

Normally, she dressed elegantly, but on this particular day, she was dressed down. She wore supermodel essentials VS graphic fleece pants, matching VS graphic hoodie, and Bailey Bow UGG boots.

"Where's ya coat?" I asked.

"In my truck," Wyoni answered.

"And where's ya truck?" I asked knowing the answer.

"In the garage."

"My garage?"

"No, Kee'! The building's garage."

I chuckled. "Whatever. Lemme have to talk to management. This is like ah breach of security...Ha ha..."

Wyoni smacked her teeth. "I wish you would call management on me," she said rearing her head back, looking over at me. "Um, Kee'?"

"What Wy'? Here we go. The real reason you came to see me...Ha, ha, ha...You always got some stuff wit' you."

"Whaaat Kee'?"

"Aw, you know, now..."

"What? Just say it."

I looked at her, "You try'na smoke, huh?"

"Yeah. My eyes are messin' wit' me...Ha," she chuckled.

"You're too much. You gon' lose ya job," I jokingly said.

"Why you keep threatening to tell on me, Kee? That ain't cool."

"No, Wy'? I ain't got no smoke.

"YES YOU DO, Kee!" Quit playin'.

"Come on, Wy'! You know I got work to do. I'm not try'na be all lazy and stuff. messin' wit' you."

"Come on, Kee', pah-leeese."

"Look...Why ain't you go to church. You need Jesus right now." We laughed.

We went to the Primanti Brothers on 18th street. Ordering their famous sandwich, we sat down to eat.

"So why didn't you come to church, I was checkin' for you," I asked Wyoni before biting into my sandwich.

"I had a long night." She couldn't even look at me when she answered.

"Oh, you got some dick last night, huh?" I asked, smiling, chewing my sandwich.

24

"Why you worried about it?!"

"Who dicked you down, Wy'?" I laughed.

"Why-y-y?!"

"Was it Graham? Did you let Graham hit it again after you told me y'all was done?"

"No!"

"No? Then who you let hit that, then? You ah li'l freak, Wy'."

"WHATEVER!"

"Yo! Spill the beans. Who was you wit'? Who made you miss church?"

"I met some guy last night."

"O-M-G, AH ONE NIGHT STAND?! You's ah freak!"

"Sshhh, shut up!" Wyoni said whispering and ducking her head down.

"I'ma say it again if you don't tell me." I wanted to know, I had to know.

"You don't know him...Hell, I don't even know him!" She chuckled. "I just needed some dick. Shit, you know I'm desperate if I take ah guy from the mall and have sex with him. It was like I went to the mall to shop for dick, but it was good. He was younger, too. He bounced up and down on this fat ass all night. He put it dah-aawn."

25

"Wy', you wild, but it is what it is," I said sipping soda through a straw.

"Who you been hittin', Kee'? Prob'ly eh'body, they mama, they sista, they aunt, and they..."

"Shut the Fa...hmph."

"Payton told me she's been trying to call you, but you ain't been answerin'. What's up wit' that?"

Aaagh, here we go again. Somebody bringing up the one I'm trying so hard to forget. Payton and Wyoni were best friends. I had introduced them to each other, and somehow they got closer than me and Wyoni were. "Come on, man..."

"I'm not ya man..."

"Shut up!"

"You shut up, Kee! Don't be mad at me cause I brought my sister up.

"Payton's not your sister, Wy'. What?! Did you forget that I introduced y'all to each other?"

"So what! That's my sister, and you need to call her back."

"Tell her to call dude, man."

"Keel?!"

"My fault, but I'm not try'na talk to her. She got ah dude. She got me going through enough stuff right now. I ain't try'na be bothered."

"And that's her fault?"

"Yeah, it is, Wy'. She cheated on me!"

There it was, the excuse for our divorce. We tried to fix things, to reconcile, but nothing worked. Not even therapy, so we separated, then we got divorced. The insane thing is she caused so much wreckage that I was still seeing our marriage counselor, six-months after the divorce. The good thing about our divorce was we didn't have kids. So no one other than ourselves were affected by our divorce, but the crazy thing was our family and friends were affected as if they were our kids.

All of us had a separate sense of being, and mines was all over the place.

Every day I thought of her, I saw her, or someone brought up my former spouse. Trying to block her out and ignore her was hard. Whatever I was feeling at the moment riding this emotional rollercoaster, I thought of scriptures that my pastor suggested, or the advice that I received from my therapist, family, and friends.

What my family and friends were going through was a state of false guilt. Because they saw us as the perfect couple. So whenever something went wrong, their impulse was to blame themselves. 'Why didn't I do this or why didn't I do that,' they asked themselves. They actually felt as though they could have prevented our divorce, but they couldn't have.

"Kee'...Kee'...KEELAN?!"

"Yeah?" Wyoni had woke me out of deep thought.

"So are you going to call her?" She asked chewing her sandwich.

"Yeah."

"When?"

"Later...I'll call her later," I said picking up my sandwich to finish it off.

"Can I be honest with you, Kee'?"

"Of course. I always want you to keep shit real with me."

"You always point your finger at Payton. It's like you don't believe you did anything wrong. Like you didn't do anything to cause yaws breakup."

"No! Wy', we both knew it was over before I caught her cheating."

"You was cheating, too!"

"I was, but only you knew that. I came to you because I was going through something. We weren't

28

having sex, we loved each other but fell out of love with each other! I mean it's so many things that played ah factor in what happened to us, and I don't know what happened to us. Why do you think I'm going to therapy? I want to learn how to love ah woman the right way. I want ah good woman, and I also want to be ah good man to ah good woman."

"Hmm, baby, I'll be ya good woman. Wit' ya sexy ass."

"Hmph," I chuckled at the stranger's advance. She was walking past us with her girlfriend, and heard what I was saying. "Oh, yeah? Thank you. But listen Wy', I'm going to call her, but I want you to quit thinking that you're going to put our marriage back together. A'ight?"

"Cool, but yaw soulmates, yaw need to get back together, or at least be friends. This not speaking, you being mad shit, ain't gon' work for neither of you."

"You right, but we gotta work this out, not you or Larry, or anybody else besides us. Feel me?"

"Yeah. You ready?"

"Yeah. Let's get outta here."

Chapter 3

SHE'S JUST AH FRIEND

Two sticks of loud and a half a bottle of wine later, I was letting Wyoni out of my loft. I had enjoyed her company and appreciated her two-cents. But work was calling, and she had to go. I know what you're thinking. You're thinking that we had sex, but we didn't. Well, we had sex a couple times years before right before we both went away to college like ten or eleven years before this.

Having sex with each other didn't work out as we planned. We thought that our friendship would blossom into a relationship after I hit that, but we were wrong. The first time we had sex was totally unexpected. I had taken her to a Mary J. concert, and somehow our lips locked us into a passionate kiss that led to hot, steamy sex. The second time we had sex was right before we went away to college. We were celebrating with friends at a bar and slid into the bathroom where we had foreplay. Then later that night, drunk, we went to her house and had unprotected sex for hours. Needless to say, a month into college, we found out that she was pregnant with my baby. With her mother helping raise her son, and us both just going away to college, we felt that her having an abortion was the best thing for us to do at that time. Shortly after the abortion, we lost contact with each other, and I found myself blocked from her social media accounts. I backed away from the situation, and I backed away from her. We both focused on our majors and future careers, and before I knew it one year had went passed, two years past then three years had went passed, and we still had not communicated with one another.

In 2005, I had gotten word that Wyoni's father had passed. She had grown up without him, but six months before his death she had located him, and tried to get answers to the questions that she had asked herself about him growing up. Watching her father's floral-covered casket descending six feet into the ground, I watched as she fell apart. Walking up to her, she turned as if knowing I would come to comfort her. Embracing me, she held me close. I could feel the hurt in her hug. Her tears were tears of mourning. She wasn't only mourning about her father, but about the child we had aborted, our child.

After several minutes, she asked for my number, and told me that we needed to talk. I agreed.

Later that night, we met at her mother's which was a place of abstinence. She wanted to give herself to me mentally and emotionally, but not physically or sexually anymore. I understood, and wanted to get to the bottom of her shutting me out of her life.

A few minutes of awkward silence elapsed between the two of us before I broke the silence. "Are you a'ight?" I asked, reaching out to hug her.

"Yeah, I guess. How have you been, Keelan. I missed you," he said somewhat smothered by my rapture.

Breaking our demonstration of affection, we found ourselves holding hands. The fact of the matter was, we missed each other.

"Come on let's sit down and talk. We have so much to catch up on," Wyoni said taking a seat in one of the porch chairs. I sat next to her on the lounger. It had been so long. We had gone from being with each other every day to not seeing or talking to one another in years. Where would we begin?

"Look Wy', I'ma just come out and ask, why did you cut me off? Why you block me, I mean, I love you, nah mean. Shit hurts." My face expressed the agony I felt inside. My bottom lip quivered. I tried to hold myself together but the question broke me into little pieces. My vulnerability made Wyoni let her guard down.

She reached over, and placed her hand atop of mine. "I was hurt and disappointed. We were young, I was confused and I was mad at you. Pick an excuse, Kee'. Mainly, I needed you to be there when I got the abortion."

"I couldn't afford to. I struggled to get the abortion money together. I had to borrow money off of ah drug dealer."

"That drug dealer was ya brother, Kee'. He would have given you more money. Look, I just needed you there. No one was. I needed you to share the blame."

"I do, Wy," I said looking over at Wyoni. We were both in tears. "I'm sorry," I stretched my arm across the back of her neck, she moved towards me, and rested her tearful face on my chest.

"I still haven't told anyone," she said, but it did not surprise me.

"Me neither," I said.

She looked up into my eyes and the moment was intense. Truth be told I was ashamed of myself, but that didn't mean that she was ashamed of herself. I don't know what her reasons were for keeping our secret and I didn't want to question her about it.

"I wanted to keep the baby," she told me in a low-whisper.

"Me too. Under different circumstances we would have," I assured her.

Again, she lifted her head from my chest, and looked up into my eyes, this time checking for sincerity. An hour had passed, I stood with her outside of my car, we embraced for the last time that night.

Driving home, I felt a sense of relief. Would we be as close as we once were? I doubted that, but I wanted to remain as close to her as I possibly could be. All that night I tossed and turned. Hearing the creaking sounds my apartment made during the late night hours made me cover my head with my pillow. It was the excuse I needed to blame my insomnia on. Peeking out from under my pillow, I stared at the time. The red glowing digits read 2:57 am on my digital alarm clock. Wide awake, I reached for my smartphone and checked my Facebook page. Not able to get Wyoni out of my mind, I closed the app, and analyzed her situation, her life as I knew it.

Wyoni was raised in a single parent home, in a household of four, her mother, herself, and two siblings. At fourteen, she was pregnant and became a teen mom at fifteen. So as a child she was forced to make an adult decision and that decision was life changing. Then during her first month of mature achievement, she was forced to make another life-altering decision, yet again. Both decisions concerning her children. Her sexual acts were forms of rebellion, and a cry for attention while seeking the love of a male. All which were misguided and not premeditated, but still damaging. Because of her hurt she wanted to address the cause of pain by addressing a male figure. And in doing so, she mistook sex as love, and a male child as a man. Robbed of her innocence and childhood, her promiscuity forced her into adulthood.

As a mislead child, she had sex with multiple partners and had become pregnant by one of them which one she didn't know. After having two teenagers take paternity test, she still didn't know who her son's father was. Deciding not to go through anymore embarrassment, she stopped pursuing the father of her child, and her decision would not only hurt her, but her son as well.

Wyoni had developed a pattern of decision making that continually stricken her, but the decision she made during our first month of college wasn't solely her decision. It was mines too. Wyoni not knowing the father of her child and me not being there during the abortion was a reminder of her father's rejection. But this form of rejection didn't just affect her, it affected her son, and our unborn child.

As a mother, she felt like a failure because as a mother she was not only supposed to be the provider, but she's also supposed to be the protector. She could never be the father, so her protection was limited as a single parent, and this made her resent men. Why did she feel like a failure? Well, because she knew that she would not be able to prevent her son from eventually being hurt because of his father abandoning him. She knew what the feeling of growing up without a father felt like, and knew that her children would feel the same way growing up without their father.

As a boy growing into a man, her son would question where his father was. Ultimately, her son would realize that parenthood didn't consist of a grandmother and a mother, but a father and a mother. The pattern of absent men in her and her son's lives, psychologically to her, meant that men weren't shit, but a phenakistoscope of men entering and exiting her life again and again. Eventually, she would hate men, and her son seeing how men had hurt her, may end up making a part of him hate men too. Sad thing is he will grow up to be the symbol of his mother's hate.

In Wyoni's book, men weren't dependable because she never had a man that she could depend on, and they definitely weren't lovable because she knew what it felt like to love a child which was unconditional. Inside of her head, she believed that a loving parent would never leave their child or deny paternity. She believed that if men were loving creatures when she got pregnant with her son the ones that had sex with her would have lined up to claim their son. She felt like she should not have had to go searching for the father. What she didn't take into account as a teenager is the father of her son was not a man at all, but a child himself.

As an adult, I did not know that I was being held accountable for every man that had let her down, and abandoned her. Unbeknownst to me, I was the only man that could change her perspective on men. I was the only man in her life that she could depend on, the only man that she could trust, and was willing to love. But when it came to the ultimate man test which was being a father, I had failed like every other man in her life before me.

Wyoni had even compromised. She had told herself if I stood by her side during the abortion, she would forgive all men. Sadly enough, I was the only man that could restore her faith in men, and I had failed us all.

37

There were two good things that came out of Wyoni's situation that instilled a certain strength in her. One was based upon her mother's support. She had a strong, black mother that supported

her no matter what and would have supported her if she had decided to keep our child. I believe deep down inside that the reason she shut me out of her life was because I forced her to make a decision that she didn't want to make. Because she loved and respected me, she surrendered her authority of choice to me, and I made the wrong choice. I'm not afraid to admit it, and I regret the fact that I told her to terminate the pregnancy.

During our conversation at her mother's house that night I realized that her decision was not her decision at all, but it was solely mines. I decided it was best for us not to have the child, not her. She just went along with me. She would have dealt with being pregnant in college, and her mother would have helped take care of our child while we were away at college. Wyoni's mother never placed blame and was always there for her daughter and grandson. This helped mold Wyoni into the strong woman she was.

The other good thing that came out of Wyoni's situation was she was able to turn her hurt and pain into love. She was able to share her experiences with the youth. She was able to explain how to

overcome the challenges of being raised in a single parent home. She was able to give advice to teen moms, and give young, black males the guidance and love they deserved.

So I had fucked up. I had forced her to make a choice that was based on my selfishness. And that choice had placed me in the same category of all the men that had left her and her children alone.

See, what Wyoni was thinking was if I didn't want the baby then her second child would also grow up being raised by a single parent and without a father. Because she felt like if she would have gone against my decision I would have instantly removed myself from her and our child's life. And as time went on she became angry with herself for not taking that chance. I remember one day she had asked me what would I have done if she would have kept the baby, and I told her that I would have had to just man the fuck up. But she had asked this question too late, and shortly after that conversation is when she started avoiding me and had transferred her anger from herself to me.

That's me and Wyoni's history. So no, we didn't have sex and probably will never have sex again. But we will forever be friends. Locked into the "friend zone," the "brother and sister zone," that zone that prohibits sex.

Does Payton know all of this? No, she doesn't. It just never came up, and neither, Wyoni, or myself, felt as though the fine details of our relationship were important. Especially since we were not planning on ever being intimate again.

Finally, able to attend to my work, I gave my Amazon Echo a voice command, "John Coltrane," and Favorite Things began to play. After cutting the end of my Davidoff torpedo, I lit it and put it between my lips, then put my small torch to it some more. Inhaling, I tilted my head back, and exhaled smoke into the air. It had been a long day, and I still had a lot of work to do. Wyoni had set me back a few hours, now it was time to play catch up. As Senior Editor of the Corridor, I not only had to do my work, but I had to check other's work as well. I had a long night ahead of me.

Sitting at my workstation, I unfolded my Mac, and opened the file titled, "Mental Issues."

I yawned, stretched my arms to the ceiling, then placed my fingers back on the keyboard of my Mac, and continued to edit and spellcheck my article on mental health. Tired, my eyes fought to close. I was a few minutes away from losing the battle, fatigue began to settle in, and I felt my body relaxing. The closer I got to finishing my work the sleepier I got.

"Okay," I said, closing my Mac, and falling back on to the headboard of my bed. I wanted to shut my eyes and fall into oblivion, but I needed to shower. I had not thoroughly washed myself since having sex with Clarissa. She, and several others, including Wyoni, tried to contact me. Some had even left messages. I didn't have the time to call anyone or check any of my messages, I was too busy trying to meet my deadline.

Gathering myself, I stood up, unbuttoned my dress shirt, threw it on my bed, then unbuckled my belt, unbuttoned and unzipped my dress pants, and let them hit the floor.

I picked my phone up from off of my bed, headed to the kitchen, then checked it to see if there were any text messages that needed my immediate attention.

TEXT MESSAGES:

Elaine at 6:47pm: Hey baby, call me I wanna know if you want to catch a movie.

Teal at 8:23pm: Where are you, Keelan? Call me when you get this message.

Clarissa at 8:34pm: I knew you weren't gonna call me. What's going on with you, you were acting strange today.

Clarissa at 8:42pam: I know you seen my message, call me.

Clarissa at 8:48pm: CALL ME!!!

Mereza at 11:27pm: I'm dying to see you, Mr. Keelan.

Picture message sent from Mereza at 12:01am: I want you.

Picture message sent from Mereza at 12:03am: Do you want me?

Picture message sent from Mereza at 12:15am: Let's play.

Wiping my face with my right hand, I gazed at the sexy pictures Mereza had sent me. They were all pictures of various body parts. Her legs, cleavage in a sexy lace bra, and her hand tucked in her lace panties. It looked as if she was playing with herself.

Sitting my phone down on my kitchen counter, I thought of me and Mereza's last encounter. She was a successful business woman that liked rough sex. Looking into my frig', my eyes searched for something to snack on. I settled for a cold cut sandwich, and a glass of orange juice.

Sitting at my kitchen counter, I bit into my sandwich, thinking of the revealing pictures Mereza had sent.

42

Deciding to play her game, I sent her a picture that revealed my defined six pack, and waited for a response.

"Unnn…nnn...nnn," my phone vibrated off of the counter. I hurried to check the message.

TEXT MESSAGES:

Mereza at 2:13am: I want to see more.

Me at 2:14am: Come look, then.

Mereza at 2:15am: On my way.

Finishing my sandwich and orange juice, I rushed to take a shower. It would only take Mereza ten minutes to get to my loft.

"Hey Eubanks, I have a visitor coming...okay, thanks." I called the doorman to alert him that I was expecting someone.

Mereza Stanley was a Pittsburgh native. She owns an art and fashion boutique. She like traveling, baking, and working out. We had caught a couple concerts out of town, and she had taken me on vacation once. She was several years older, but had the body of a fitness trainer. We occasionally had sex, at least once a month. To be completely honest, I looked forward to her unexpected text messages. It had taken her a month and a half to get back at me because like I said, she traveled a lot.

TEXT MESSAGES:

Me to Mereza 2:22am: The doorman knows you're coming. Come up, the door's open.

Headed to the shower, I left a trail of under garments. My socks, boxers, and wife-beater led to my bathroom. I wanted to take a shower and make sure every crevice of my body was clean. Mereza liked to use her tongue to tickle me in the strangest places. Living on the Northside, she was only several minutes away, so I showered in a hurry.

Ten minutes after me getting into the shower, Mereza, made her entrance, ready to go. She came dressed in a three-quarter bleached mink coat with a natural fox trim. Underneath was a black see-through bra and pantie set. Her hair was in a slicked-back pony with a frizzled, curly tail, and her feet were in a pair of eighteen-hundred dollar Tom Ford sandals. With the stream of water sprouting out of the showerhead in repetitious jabs, hitting my face, I never heard her enter. Turning the shower off, I exited the small, glass cubicle, and there she was.

Mereza stood at the bathroom door with my towel dangling from her finger, "Come and get it."

Her statement was innuendo, and I wanted her to be clear about what she was referring to. "What? The towel or you?"

"You decide."

"Oh yeah?!"

"Yeah!" She said with a sly smile on her face, her hand on her hip exposing her bra and panty draped body, posed like a Saks Fifth Avenue mannequin.

Not saying another word, I removed the shower cap from my head, and let my dreads fall down my back. Walking towards her, water shriveled to small beads that crawled down the naked frame of my body. My mind envisioned me fucking Mereza from the back, and my dick hardened like a concrete slab. Mereza's eyes told me that what she seen before her was pleasing and enticing.

"Mm...mm...mm," she emphasized biting down on her bottom lip. Never taking her

eyes off of my chiseled figure. She admired its structure and complexion, it's a cross between bronze and gold. My face is that of a divine being with a well-structured jawline. My silhouette is that of Black Jesus.

Dropping the towel from her finger, she reached into her mink coat pocket, and pulled out a sexual device. "Follow me."

I followed her into my bedroom as if it was hers. She stopped at the edge of the bed, holding the sexual device out in her hand with her back to me. Then she slipped out

45

of her mink, and climbed up on the bed. Slowly, she spread her legs and pulled her panties to the side. Her pussy hair was shaved clean, and her clit was pierced. Her pussy lips slightly hung and glistened from pussy juices leaking from her insides.

"What you want, huh?" I asked.

Mereza, nudged her head towards the sexual device, then down to her wet pussy.

"Hmph, you want this in there. What do I get?"

Mereza, licked two of her fingers and slowly took them into her mouth as if they were my dick.

Balling my face up, I bit my bottom lip, and haltingly shook my head up and down.

"Okay."

The sexual device was a remote controlled silver bullet, two inches of pure sexual pleasure. Before I slipped it into her pussy, I cocked my head sideways and licked the slit of her cunt, back and forth, up and down. Then flicked my tongue over her pierced clit. She took in a deep breath as if I had poured a bucket of cold water on her.

"Whew, ew, ew, ah."

Then I took the silver ball, and clicked it on, "Vrrrrrr..." It vibrated. "CLICK! Vrrrrrrr...CLICK!

VRRRRRRRRR." On level three, I gently ran it up and down her clit.

Mereza, scooted back. Her face displayed a look of erotic ecstasy, but the surge of vibration took her breath and knocked her back as if a lightning bolt had hit her. "Ooh," she finally verbalized.

"Get back here!" I demanded.

Mereza, shook her head, no.

"Get back here," I said firmly, but in a whisper.

Mereza scooted back towards me, panting, and rolling her eyes. "Take it easy on me, please," she asked.

"Uh-uhn, nope."

"Pleeaase?!"

"Nall, you shouldn't have run from me." Looking in her eyes, I licked my lips. "Put them legs on my shoulders and that pussy in my face," I told her, wrapping my arms around her thighs, locking my face into a position to eat her pussy. Licking it, I feverishly shook my head like a pit, fluctuating, caressing it with my tongue. Then I put the bullet in her pussy and went to work on her pierced clit.

"Kee...Kee...Keeee...Kee-lan...Kee-lan!   Oh,   I'm cummin'...Oh, I'm cah...Cah...Caaah-men!"

Hearing her having an orgasm made me go in more and more. Mereza, fought to get away from me, but she couldn't. My arms were wrapped tightly around her thighs as she released her juices into my mouth.

"Stop," she said, but I kept eating her pussy, "Stop...Keelan. STOP! I'm serious, stop, Keelan. I'm done."

Noticing that her stops were not sexual, enticing stops, but meaningful stops, I stopped and released her from my grip. "Are you serious? You gon' leave me like this, Mereza?"

"Next time you'll answer the first time I call ya ass."

"Fa' real? You fo' real? I was working."

"Whatever. You always say that shit," Mereza, muttered before she got dressed and walked out of my bedroom.

"Mereza, look here. Mereza...MEREZA! It's cool..It's cool. I got you." I couldn't believe what had just happened, but I would definitely make sure it would never happen again. No longer would I permit her to arouse me with electronic intimacy, to thrill me with romantic correspondences of scribbled foreplay, nor would I allow her to touch my sensitive body parts through long distant turn me ons transmitted graphically enough to make me cum!

She was a good sexter that knew how to lure me with sex messages that popped up on my smartphone's screen, pulsating through perfect phrases mixed with steamy pics underscored with a mix of deviance, little whorish words, and clichés.

Through intimate sexting I had allowed her to put an end to my seclusion. She had enticed me and used my weakness for sex as a key to enter my room of loneliness, and left it ransacked by throwing around her exploitative illustrations and provocative tag-lines used as sexual teasers.

Mereza's body had been sent into seizure-like frenzies, tantrums backed by her screams of share pleasure, and X-rated rants of, "Yes ...Yes...Yesses!" She had climaxed in ecstasy with the help of my manual labor. FUCK! I had gone to work on her to say the least, but it was all about her orgasms, not mine! Not ours! But hers!

Her ignorant ass had rebuked my tempting physical advances, god-like looks, and pic of my ripped abdominal. She had invited me to play a game of textual erotica, but it played out more like sexual roulette, and she had beat me by allowing me to play myself. The only thing that had been blown on me was my mind. "Click...Click, BANG!"

My vulnerability had been left exposed, and she was the culprit that got away.

Her multiple orgasm's had discharged into my face like a barrage of gunshots released from an automatic weapon. Her sexting was mentally graphic enough to have left a crime scene, littered with sexy lingerie, and a mechanical plaything that was still vibrating on my bed. Me, she had left me holding a fully loaded sex-pistol. My dick was hard as steel. It was stiff as if rigor mortis had set.

Cursing her, I masturbated. Well worked up, it didn't take long for me to cum. After a few minutes, my dick exploded warm semen on my defined abs. "Hmph...Ah...Ah...Ah...Mmmm," I panted feeling like a silly teenager outsmarted by a sly-trickster. Mereza pulling this stunt was like her pulling the string on Venetian Blinds. She had opened and closed the barrier between her and my soul.

After taking a shower, I found my phone, scrolled down to the name Mereza, and deleted her from my phone and my life.

Chapter 4

KEELAN'S BROTHER, "ON DECK."

Dario Rockmon or as his friend's called him, "On Deck," was considered to be some type of street gangster. On several occasions, I've heard him referred to him as an O.G. or an Original Gangster.

To my mother, he was just her loving baby boy. To me, he was just my little brother, Dorio. We were born a year a part, he was going on thirty-eight and I already was thirty-eight.

No matter what was said about Dorio or what he did, my mother always came to his aid. She truly loved her youngest son. Sometimes I believed that she loved him more than me. At times that upset me, and I allowed it to put a wedge between the two of us. It wasn't until I read the famous Parable of Jesus, the one about the Prodigal Son, did I have an understanding of my Mother's love for her lost sheep.

Jesus starts the Parable off by saying, "There was a man who had two sons... The younger brother had taken his share of his father's estate, and set off to squander his wealth in wild living. After spending every dime, he came to his senses, and returned home. His father, seeing his youngest son approaching, was filled with compassion. It didn't matter what his son did, he still loved him, and gave him the best of everything. He had even prepared a feast for him. Seeing this, the older brother felt resentment, but his father pleaded with him, saying, "Your brother was dead and he's alive again; he was lost and is found."

In my case, I was also filled with resentment whenever I felt like my mother was favoring my brother over me. But my self-centered exclusiveness had also left me lost. How could I accuse my mother of loving one of us more than the other? The reality of the matter was she loved us equally.

What made her love seem unequal was this small detail.

Me, I was a college grad, and my brother was a drug dealer. The difference between the two of us was, I was self-sufficient, and he called on her more. At times, he needed her to bail him out of jail, to do certain things for him while he was doing time, and she had even put his property in her name, so the police couldn't take it.

In realizing these things, I let go of my jealousy and resentment. I thought about all of the times my little brother had helped me out, like with the abortion situation that Wyoni and I went through. Truth be told, I loved my brother. He was the only sibling I had. I didn't agree with his lifestyle, but I had his back, regardless. So after a few prison emails, a tripped to the mall, and a dozen phone calls about his release, I made a road trip to Beaver, West Virginia.

I arrived at FCI Beckley, walked to the C.O. at the desk and handed him the package in my hand.

"Okay, I'll make sure he gets these," the C.O. at the messaging office told me taking my brother's clothes. "We should be calling him shortly."

"Rockmon, report to the message center for release...Rockman, report to the message center for release." Walking back to my truck, I heard my brother's name being paged over a loud-speaker.

Hearing his name called, Dorio "On Deck" Rockmon, dried his body off, put on his underclothes, and walked out of the shower area to his bunk.

***

The camp is different from the penitentiary. The camp is set up like a dormitory. It's like a warehouse or barracks set-up with bunkbeds.

"Come on Deck! Ya ass should've been out the shower...Dat nigga ain't try'na go home...Let me take ya place, Deck." On Deck's friend's yelled throughout the Unit.

"Naw nigga, I'm out. Ain't no ma'fucka takin' my place. I did my fuckin' time."

"You got eh'thang, Deck?" On Deck's friend and bunky, Samuel "Fishscale" Fischer, asked.

"Yeah. You know I'm good. Like I said eh'thang in the locker's yours. You can give these niggas whatever you want 'em to have. All I'm taking is my mail, pics, and Bible."

"ROCKMON, REPORT TO THE MESSAGE CENTER, NOW!" The C.O. called out again, on the P.A. system.

"Get on outta here, Deck!" One of On Deck's old heads yelled out. "Don't make them people call ya ass again."

"Don't forget about me, Deck. I need you, homie," Fishscale said embracing On Deck and shaking his hand.

"Oh fo' sho! You know I got you. I'ma take care of that right away. Plus, you know you 'bout to get out too. So I'ma hold you all the way down."

***

Waiting for my brother, I thought about all of the other young black males in his position. This was the second time my brother had served time. He did a one to three upstate, and this time he had done almost four years for a gun charge.

In doing my research for my article about America drugging kids, I had come across some eye-popping reports. Overall, black males are under attack. Growing up, I never understood another man blaming his faults on another race. I've heard my brother and others, kick around those common statements that were supposed to make up for black people's ignorance, like, "We don't got no planes to bring the drugs over here," or, "I gotta sell drugs. There ain't nothing else out here for me," and I really hated hearing four hundred years of oppression being stated as the reason why we, as a people, fall behind, and don't accomplish our goals.

But after looking over some things, I came to realize that there was one factor that affected the black households of America, and that was trauma. There's a cycle of trauma that black males go through growing up that leads to PTSD, and giving their disproportionate knowledge, the DHS doesn't have a clue about what goes on in the 'hood, so to say. DHS can't come up with up with a solution that will resolve the mental issues black kids develop witnessing their peers getting murdered, neglect, and the lack of fundamental relationships with their parent's that causes an emotional reaction to hurt deep.

Childhood trauma and years of bouncing from home to home is some of the simplest causes of a child's distress, and nuanced solutions for dealing with such trauma can be limited in schools. The prognosis for the aggression that comes about through black youths is defined as ADHD which leads to our children being legally drugged with antipsychotics and SGAs.

Truthfully speaking, medication may interrupt the immediate behavior, but it doesn't begin to address the pain black kids are in. Using pills to sedate a child with disruptive behavior often obscures the actual cause of the child's vexation. America's resolution for dealing with uppity negroes is to kill them, lock them up, drug them, or send them to foster care.

In fact, since the Protection Legislation was passed following the Sandusky Scandal, the number of youth in foster care, infants to age 21, has soared, and antipsychotic use is four times higher among foster children than among other Medicaid enrolled kids that were diagnosed with ADHD. The duration of antipsychotic use in foster kids is larger than it is for those not in foster care. White youths are twenty-seven percent less likely than black youths to receive an antipsychotic in conjunction with another drug.

One of the saddest things about this is DHS has no data of how many children in America that are receiving behavioral health care services, and there is no study that shows that medicating kids with behavioral issues long term, will help or not.

So under the surface of these excuses used by blacks in America, is a fact that leads to a lackluster performance in our race. And my brother, like many other blacks in America, suffer from the effects from Post-Traumatic Stress Disorder that growing up in the 'hood causes.

As I thoroughly gave thought to one of America's many injustices, my brother emerged from the belly of the beast. Seeing him walking to me, I exited my truck, and stood outside of it with a smile on my face. "What's up, bro?"

"What's up wit' you?"

Before I could respond, we were hugging each other. This time my hug was tighter than the others. I wished I could have been as strong as my little brother. Holding him made me happy. We finally had my brother back. When I say we, I mean my mother, his daughter, and myself. I wasn't just happy for myself, but for them as well. My mother had been there for him every single day, and now he was able to ride home with me.

"Damn bro, it's so good to have you back," I said mesmerized by his muscular body frame.

"Where's ya stuff?" I asked looking down at the letters, pictures, and Bible he was holding, "That's it?"

"Yeah, bro. I left the rest of that shit. I don't need no reminders," my brother answered walking to the passenger side to get in the truck.

"You know Ma was try'na ride up with me?" I told my brother.

"I bet she was. She's funny as hell," my brother said looking at my truck. "Damn, I'm finally outta dat bitch, bro. Yo, dis dat article you was telling me about? I ain't get to read it. You know with getting out, I had my hands full an' shit."

"Yeah, the one about America drugging our children," I replied pulling out of FCI Beckley's parking lot.

The Corridor Article: WE THE PEOPLE DRUGGING THE RED, WHITE AND BLUE CHILDREN OF AMERICA:

As the government of the United States aims its focus on Mexico capturing the world's most notorious drug lord, and tallies up its numbers of drug overdoses driving up the death rate of white adults 25-to-34, they ignores the fact that they have their own El Chapo to deal with.

Alex Gorsky, the CEO of Johnson & Johnson, the makers of the white powdery substance called Baby Powder, and other child care products, are also the makers of the SGA Risperdal, a drug that increases hormonal prolactin and causes the bodies of both boys and girls to mimic pregnancy.

Earlier this year, an Autistic young man was rewarded $2.5 million in damages, after years of treatment with Risperdal for his behavior problems and he developed size 46 DD breast.

Recently as 2014, the U.S. Food and Drug Administration (FDA), the ones responsible for approving drugs and treatment, stated that Risperdal is an important and beneficial therapeutic option for children and adolescents facing very challenging mental illnesses and neurodevelopmental disorders, in support of the pharmaceutical kingpin, Alex Dorsky.

Meanwhile Johnson & Johnson has spent $3 billion to settle thousands of cases-both civil and criminal-involving promotion of Risperdal by it's-middleman- company, Janssen, their pharmaceutical entity. Despite the fact that powerful antipsychotic drugs are turning our children into X-Men like mutants, that suffer from side effects of illness, weight gain, and disorientation, we are still allowing doctors to prescribe them and pharmaceutical companies supply them.

"Dat's right, bro, get 'em!"

"Hmph," I looked over and watched as my brother took in the article.

"While drug stings by undercover Federal Agents seize huge volumes of controlled substances, and harsh policies like Mandatory Minimums, are being handed down to tens of thousands of non-violent offenders, America overlook other drug peddlers like doctors and DHS healthcare providers drugging our children with powerful psychiatric medication that can barely be managed by adults, but yet, are being provided to the very young. Some as young as four years old.

Stimulants like Ritalin, and other Second Generation Antipsychotic drugs like Adderall, nicknamed "Kiddie Cocaine," Risperdal, Zyprexa, Tardive Dyskinesia (TD), and Seroquel are SGAs that causes life-threatening side effects like incredibly fast obesity, major hormonal and metabolic changes to the brain, fatigue, perennial congestion, constipation, headaches, mouth sores, involuntary movements of the tongue, limbs, jaws and torso, incessant lip-smacking, bladder problems that could lead to them being catheterized, and kids between the ages 10 and 18 taking antipsychotics are 50 percent more likely to develop diabetes."

"Damn, bro, dis shit's deep," my brother commented looking up from the article.

"The most recent available numbers suggest that 750,000 kids in the U.S. are on antipsychotics, and most of the time, children and adolescents get these drugs "Off-label" not for psychosis, but for common problems like ADHD, for which these drugs are not approved.

The drugs given to kids in juvenile facilities, schools, and foster homes are generally approved for the drugs. Many of the children and adolescents diagnosed with Schizophrenia, some type of bipolar disorder, and irritability related to Autism, are treated with these medications.

In many of these cases, a DHS health care provider suggested a child needed to be on these heavy psychotic medications instead of a temporary stimulant or other non-medicinal method. The doctor was actually initiating antipsychotics. The recommendation was less about children getting antipsychotics in dire circumstances, and more about prescribing a chemical restraint that would cause dangers to the child's developing brain.

In America, antipsychotic prescriptions for children and youths have grown at a greater rate than those for all other psych drugs, including other stimulants.

In 2014 alone, almost 20,000 antipsychotic prescriptions were written for children two or younger, a 50 percent increase from 2013. So as pharmaceutical giants like Johnson & Johnson get richer and richer off of a medical violation that's equal to the Tuskegee Syphilis Study, our children, particularly, minorities, and vulnerable kids in juvenile detention centers and foster care system are walking around in society disoriented, overmedicated, overweight, and twitchy.

As of 2009, Rutgers researchers discovered 12.4 percent of foster kids were taking these sedating medications, compared with 1.4 percent of children who were on Medicaid, but not in foster care and only one percent of kids with private insurance were prescribed these same medications.

"Bro, you really did ya thing with this article," my brother told me, folding the paper and throwing it in the back seat. "Did you see that Doc: Prison Kids?" My brother asked.

"Yes. I believe it was because of some of the things exposed on that documentary that President Obama stopped solitary confinement in juvenile detention."

"The one kid spent 229,000 hours in solitary confinement."

"That's crazy. They said Florida incarcerates kids at a higher rate than any other state."

"Yeah, and dat judge...Yo, he said he locked up the most kids. He was lockin' they asses up."

"Yeah, but then he realized what he was doing was wrong. It's like he had an epiphany...ha ha ha..."

"Ha...ha, yeah, but now his program is helping the kids. And some of dem ma'fuckas need help."

"But not all of them need to be doped up."

"You right," my brother said with a subtle nod. "You see dat seven-year-old boy..."

"Zion?"

"Yeah, his 'lil ass was so bad he took medication, and said a prayer to help his ass...ha ha ha..."

"Ha...ha, yeah bro, that was wild as hell. But it was love and care, a medication that don't cost a thing, that helped him. Love is what changed the heart of that judge...Speaking of children, when's the last time you talked to Doraine?" Doraine is my niece, my brother's daughter.

"Like ah couple of days ago. I can't stand her fuckin' mother, fuck dat bitch! She so worried about suckin' ah niggas dick, and goin' out an' shit. Bitch brought my daughter to see me like five times."

63

"Well, me and ma made sure you saw her as much as we could."

"I know, an' good look, but I'm just sayin'..."

"What? If it wasn't for her, we wouldn't have been able to bring her at all. She could've put ah stop to all of that, bro."

"Yeah right! I would've killed dat bitch!"

"Bro, you just got out, we ain't even in Pittsburgh yet, and you talkin' 'bout killin' somebody. You sure you ready to be out here?"

"What da fuck you mean, bro?!"

"I'm just sayin', what happened to all of that church talk. You came outta the jail with ah Bible in ya hand, and you talkin' all this nigga this, nigga that...Bitch this, bitch that, and you gon' kill somebody. What da fuck is wrong wit' you?!"

"Smck!" My brother smacked his teeth, and looked at me sideways. "Nigga, you can miss me with all dis self-righteous shit. I'm saved and believe in Jesus Christ, but we all got our faults, an' shit. You ain't no better than me."

"Bra, I ain't on no self-righteous shit. I'm just try'na save my brother. You see the papers I've been sending you. Guys like you are dying eh'day, rapidly. Mainly because they walk around with the same self-destructive attitude you got."

"Fuck you. I ain't try'na hear dat shit." My brother turned from me and started staring out of the window. I could tell I had struck a nerve.

"I mean, you try'na blame that woman for you gettin' locked up."

"Nigga, dat bitch knew what was goin' on. She played her part in what I was doin', and to be real wit' you, they was try'na give her this charge. But I ain't no sucka ass nigga, I ate dis shit. So I feel like she should've played her part. The bitch spent my money, got my car, but she couldn't help me do dis time, fuck her! Oh, an' I forgot to mention the bitch had a baby by ah nigga from the 'hood...Pittsburgh! Dat's what I'm talkin' 'bout. I ain't try'na hear this shit."

Seeing the Pittsburgh exit, helped my brother end our discussion about his attitude, but I wasn't done with him. I wasn't going to give up on him. I wanted to save him, and prevent him from doing any more time. My mother was getting older, and she might not survive another one of his prison bids.

Fifteen minutes later, we were pulling up to my mother's Swissvale home.

"I know mom's gon' be happy as hell to see me," my brother said as I put the key in the front door and opened it.

"SURPRISE!!" The small group of family and friends yelled out, startling my brother.

"DAAADDY! Daddy!" His daughter screamed, running up to hug him.

My brother hugged her, picked her up, and swung her around, "Hey, daddy's princess," he said as her mother walked up to them. The room got quiet.

"Hi Deck," she said.

My brother put his daughter down and hugged her mother. "All that shit he was talking," is all I said to myself as we smiled at each other.

"Okay now, where's my sugar...Where's my love?"

My mother stepped up to my brother, and opened her arms to take him into her bosom.

"Aw ma, you know you can get it."

"Baby I made you ah nice brunch," my mother told my brother. And there it was, just like in the Bible, the return of the Prodigal Son.

Chapter 5

SHADY BROADS

It was 5:05 am on a Thursday. Lying in my bed, my mind raced, flashing thought after thought. I was telling myself to get up, but my body wasn't complying. I thought about the things I had to do such as meet with my pastor. There were a few things going on with my life that I need to better manage. He suggested that I come and see him for a counseling session, and I agreed to it. I also had to withdraw $5000.00 from the bank for my brother. Other than that, my day was pretty much open.

Sitting up in my bed, I reached for the remote, and turned on my TV. There was my ex-wife. It was crazy that we were no longer together, but I was still waking up to her.

"I'm Payton Crawford-Rockmon, and this is BNN." Her keeping my last name was part of our settlement agreement. She practically walked away with very little. But my last name was one of those little things.

Looking at Payton reminded me of how beautiful she was. After a few minutes of watching her talk about the Presidential Candidate, Donald Trump, I made my way to my kitchen with my Mac in hand.

There was something pleasant about waking up alone, but it also had its disadvantages. There wasn't a nagging voice shattering the morning's quietness, but there was no morning sex either.

After making me a cup of morning Joe, I sat at my kitchen counter watching the snow fall. "Echo, temperature for Pittsburgh."

Echo: "Snow shower...High: 31°...Low: 19°."

As my Amazon Echo told me the temperature, I walked to my window and was surprised by the snow's accumulation, "Damn." I thought not wanting to deal with the snow, let alone the crazed drivers of Pittsburgh. But I had things to do.

"Bro, can I please hold five stacks. I can't get to my money right now." I heard my brother's voice sounding off in my head. I halfway smiled, wondering how much money my brother had stashed Then I wondered where his stash was at, "I can't get to my money right now." I heard him say again.

Shaking my head, I shook-off the thought of my brother using my money to do something foolish. Either way, I had to come through for him.

I believed our talk had some impact on him. That was one thing about my brother. He gave you a hard time when you told him about himself, but he always evaluated what was said, and took well to constructive-criticism.

After having brunch with our mother, he left with his daughter, and her mother, Karima Black.

Karima was okay, but she could do some scandalous shit at times. But overall, she was a decent woman. Before she had two kids, she had a tight body. During my brother's incarceration she had gained a few pounds, whether it was because of stress or baby-fat, I didn't know. Regardless, she was a beautiful sister, and I loved her. So did my mother. Thinking about her, I wondered how my brother would adjust to her new baby. The baby she had conceived with his homie.

Eventually, I wanted to have kids, but first I had to settle down. Maybe I would marry again, maybe not. I didn't know what I was doing relationship wise. I hoped that Pastor Pops Thomas could give me divine guidance.

Within the last several days, I had been sexually involved with two women, and pursued by several others. Sitting there with my cup of coffee keeping me company, I flipped open my MacBook Pro, and checked my Instagram and Facebook page. I had over seventy messages.

I had posted an excerpt of my Article, and had received over twelve-hundred likes, and a few hundred comments. After I liked a few comments I read, I scanned my Inbox. I went through my messages looking for names I knew, and clicked on the name Clarissa. She had sent me a picture message of a white teddy bear holding a heart with the words, I Miss You, written at the bottom of the picture.

FACEBOOK INBOX:

Keelan to Clarissa: Miss you too. What time you get off. Maybe we can catch a bite to eat.

Clarissa to Keelan: Getting ready for work now. I get off at four, I'll be home around five. And I would love to see you later.

Keelan to Clarissa: I'll call you around 7:00 pm.

Clarissa to Keelan: Alright.

Her sending the words, "I Miss You," was like her telling me she loved me. Just like the words, I would love to see you, was her way of telling me she wanted me. I asked her about going to eat, and her response was, I can't wait to see you, translation, I can't wait to fuck you.

Closing my Inbox with Clarissa, I scrolled down and clicked on the name, Elaine. Inside of our Inbox, I clicked on her name that was colored in blue, and was sent to her page.

Elaine's measurements were 32C-25-42, she was born and raised in Mississippi, but had relocated to Pittsburgh pursuing a job opportunity. She road motorcycles, loved to ski, and travel. Looking at her short, sexy ass in her pictures, made me want to have sex with her.

Like...Like...Like...Like...Like...Like...I liked several of her pictures, just to let her know that I had stopped by her page. A minute or so later, she Inboxed me.

FACEBOOK INBOX:

Elaine to Keelan: ☹

Keelan to Elaine: Why the sad face?

Elaine to Keelan: You don't like me anymore.

Keelan to Elaine: Yes I do. ☺

Elaine to Keelan: Prove it.

Keelan to Elaine: How?

Elaine to Keelan: I'm off today. Come over for breakfast.

Keelan to Elaine: I gotta go to the bank at 9.

Elaine to Keelan: See, you playin'. It's only going on six. You can come over before you go to the bank. ☺

Keelan to Elaine: I'll be over in ah half. ☺

Elaine to Keelan: ☺

Closing my Inbox with Elaine, I scrolled down my messages and clicked on the name Teal and opened her message.

FACEBOOK INBOX:

Teal to Keelan: So you fuck me once, and say fuck me, huh?!

Her message made me feel bad. This was not what I was trying to convey to her. For some reason Elaine and I didn't click. I was losing interest in Clarissa and I had cut Mereza off, but I really liked Teal. She owned a Lady's Boutique called, *Click Your Heel's*. It wasn't just about sex with her. If I was to settle down with any of the women I was messing with, it would be with her. She also was a member of our church. I had met her during Tuesday night Bible Study. Busy with work and running errands for my brother, made me miss Bible Study this week. That, plus me not returning her calls or messages, probably is what had her feeling this way.

Keelan to Teal: Sorry I haven't been in touch. I had a deadline to meet, and my brother just got out of jail, so I've been tied up. Forgive me for not calling you back. I'll make it up to you this weekend. Hit me when you get this message.

After sending my message, I waited for Teal to respond. Checking the last time, she had logged in, I figured that she wouldn't get back to me until later.

Closing my Macbook, I headed to the bathroom where I brushed my teeth, gargled and showered. "Women, man's biggest downfall," I thought. Soaping up my muscular body, I grew an erection thinking about how good Elaine's pussy was.

***

"He's on his way here now. I'll text you when he gets here. He gone tear this shit up...How long is it gon' take for you to get over here?" Elaine was talking to her friend, Leslie, on her smartphone.

"I'm still at work. I get off at eight. I'll come straight over after work."

"That's good. That'll give me time to get me some of that dick."

"Girl, ya ass is crazy."

"Shit! That boy can fuck. I've been feindin' fo' that ding-a-ling."

"Ha…ha…ha, guurrlll. You're ah mess…What kind of car he got?"

"Hm…hm… ha…ha…ha…He gotta, hm…Ah silver Land Rover."

"Laine, why you doin' this to him?"

"Cause he's ah liar, and I hate lying ass ma'fuckas. He tried to tell me that he gotta go to the bank, and shit. He hookin' up with another bitch. I ain't stupid."

"Hmph, I hate ah lyin' ma'fucka too. I don't know why niggas always be try'na play ah bitch…You better get me outta jail, if I get caught."

"You ain't gon' get caught. Just make sure you park ya car up the street when you do it."

"Oh, I am. I ain't dumb, bitch. I busted ah couple niggas shit out before."

"I know that's why…"

Knock! Knock! Knock!

"I called ya ass," Elaine fnished saying. Hearing a knock at her door, she paused, mid-sentence. "He's here, girl."

"Kay, I'll be over." Leslie told Elaine before hanging up.

"Hey, Keelan," Elaine said letting Keelan into her house. "I need ah hug." Elaine told Keelan, opening up her arms to him. "Mmmmm," she moaned caressing his back.

"Shit smells good. What you cooking me?" I asked breaking the embrace Elaine and I shared.

"French toast with strawberries, sausage, and eggs. How you want'cha eggs?"

"Scrambled."

"You want apple juice or orange juice?"

"Orange," I replied, checking my vibrating phone.

"Mmm-hm, bitch calling him now," Elaine thought seeing me check my phone. But my brother was texting me.

TEXT MESSAGE:

On Deck to Keelan 6:37 am: Bro, this Deck. You still got me?

Keelan to On Deck 6:37 am: Going to the bank at 9.

   I'll hit you soon as I leave the bank.

On Deck to Keelan 6:38 am: Good look!

Keelan to On Deck 6:38 am: Don't mention it.

"So you gotta go to the bank at nine o'clock, huh?" Elaine asked.

"Yeah, that was my brother right there asking me if I was going."

"Oh, I ain't know you had ah brother," Elaine said. "You's ah lyin' ass malfucka," she said in a whisper.

"Huh?" I swore I heard her call me ah liar.

"Nothing, I just didn't know you had ah brother," Elaine said. "What's his name?"

"His friends call him Deck or On Deck. I posted a pic of me, him, and my mom on my page. You ain't see it?" I asked.

"Nope," Elaine said. "Lying ass, I ain't see no picture cause ain't no picture," she said in a whisper.

"Huh?" Did she just say there is no picture I thought to myself.

"Nothing," she replied scrambling my eggs.

"Kiss...Kiss...Kiss," I walked up behind Elaine as she was cooking, pressed my semi-hard dick against the crease of her ass, and kissed her on her neck.

"Yes baby, put that dick on this ass."

Elaine was wearing a black negligee, a pink silk robe, and fluffy, pink slippers. As I kissed her on the neck, I reached my hand around her to play with her pussy.

"Aaaagh..."

"You like that," I asked, working my fingers in circles around her clit.

"You gon' have me burn ya eggs, baby."

"Fuck it burn 'em."

"Ha ha ha, you crazy. Sit down, let me feed you, then fuck you," Elaine said to me pushing her fat ass back towards me. Her head was cocked to the side. She moaned as I sucked on her neck. "Why don't you hang out with me today. I'll take to you to meet my brother. Maybe, I'll even take you shopping. I don't have to work until later," I lied wanting to make room on my schedule for Teal.

"You gon' let me hang with you," Elaine turned around to face me, and asked.

"Smck...Smck...Smck," I pecked her on the lips a few times before I answered. "Yes, why wouldn't I?"

"Because you going to the bank was supposed to be a lie. You're supposed to be hooking up with another woman." Elaine thought. "I don't know, you just surprised me with that," she said.

"Well, you can ride along if you want to. I have to meet with my pastor in ah few hours, but we can hang out until then."

"Okay, Kee'. I'm so happy. I just be wanting to spend time with you," Elaine said wrapping her arms around my neck, and giving me a peck on the lips.

"I know, I just be busy," I said with my arms wrapped around her waist, gripping her fat ass.

"Sit down, baby. Let me serve you." Elaine told me to sit down, so I took a seat at her kitchen table.

She prepared my plate and sat it in front of me. "Go 'head and eat, I'll be right back." She told me, pulling her cell out of her robe pocket to make a call.

"Yeah, tell him you can't be with him 'cause we're hangin' out today," I joked.

"I'm not calling a man. I got the man I want sitting in my kitchen," Elaine patronized me.

"Yeah right!" I thought. "You're just saying that," I said between bites of my food.

"No! For real!" Elaine said dialing her friend Leslie's cell. She had a change of heart. But Leslie's cell was dead, and she had left her charger at home.

"Damn!" Elaine exclaimed, trying her friend's cell again. "This is Leslie, I am unavailable..." Elaine hung up the phone, hearing her friend's cell go straight to her voicemail service.

"Come on, Elaine. You're supposed to be feeding me. Is this how you treat the man that's taking you shopping...okay, that's it, you're just getting a pair of socks outta me, nothing else."

"Yeah right," she yelled back at me. "Here I come...Come on Les', answer the damn phone." Leslie's voice service came over the line, this time Elaine left a message. "Bitch, never mind. He wasn't lying. The nigga's takin' me shoppin' an' eh'thang. Don't do nothing to his shit. Call me back."

"Yo! Elaine?!"

"Here I come Kee," she answered walking back into the kitchen. Elaine put her cell back into her robe pocket. "Give me the fork big baby." She said taking the fork out of my hand. I smiled at her, it felt good to be served. "Matter of fact, feed yourself," Elaine said, changing the smile on my face. "I want some dick, bad!" She said, trying to unloosen my pants. She had put a smile right back on my face as I helped her get my pants and boxers down."

"You want some of this big sausage, huh?" I asked Elaine, but she didn't say a word. She just looked up at me, stroking my dick with a sinful grin on her face. She licked her lips, and took my baby maker in her mouth as I leaned back in my chair.

79

After a few minutes of her sucking, slurping, and moaning, she took me into her bedroom, but before we made it to the bed she pushed me against the wall, and fell to her knees where she continued to give me head. The more she sucked, slurped, moaned, and jacked me off while doing so, the weaker my knees got. Then she led me to the bed. With my back to the edge of it, she shoved me onto it.

After taking off her silky robe, she slipped her negligee over her head, and let it fall to the floor. Pantiless, she climbed on top of me. "Keep your hands above ya fuckin' head, don't touch me, or I'ma stop," she commanded. Then she tongued my ear, nibbled on my earlobe, kissed down my neck, circled my right nipple with her wet tongued, and talked filthy little words to me as she did it. My heart rate increased. It started beating faster and faster. I even started breathing heavier and heavier, watching her intensify our sexual encounter.

"Ah...Ah...Ah...Uh...Uh," she had me panting as she stroked me faster and faster. Then she ran her tongue down the center of my muscular abs until my dick found seclusion in the cavity of her warm mouth. After getting my meat poker as hard as she believed she could get it, she laid atop of me. I tried to use my hands to enter her, but she grabbed me by the wrist, and forcefully held my hands above my head as she pressed herself against me. The closeness of our bodies caused a friction that was electric. Hot and horny, she straddled my thigh and grinded on it until she came, leaving me begging. "Let me put it in," over and over.

The wetness of her pussy made the mouth of my penis drool a glazing her mouth would enjoy to taste. Finally, her small, soft hands took a hold of my swollen manhood, and position her body to take it all in. Damn. As her dripping dick taker covered my sex pole, I wanted to yell about how good her foreplay was, how hot her pussy was, and how warm her mouth was.

Urnk! Urnk! Urnk! Urnk! Urnk!

"No!" The sound of a car alarm interrupted my orgasm. "Oh shit! That's my truck!" I yelled instead of the erotic soundtrack that came along with me cumming. Lifting Elaine off of me, I rushed to get to my vehicle.

"No, it's not! My neighbor's car alarm goes off all the time!" Elaine tried to convince me to stay, but I know the sound of my shit.

Slipping on my clothing items, I rushed outside with my truck keys in my hand. "Bleep-bleep," it cried. "Fuck

Leslie!" I immediately grabbed my cell out of my front pocket to call 911.

Elaine felt a sense of disappointment in herself, but blamed her friend because she didn't answer when she called her to abort the mission. Slipping on some clothes, she went outside after Kee to see the damage Leslie had done to his truck.

"What the fuck!" I said. I was hot. My windshield was busted, my driver-side window was shattered, and 'Fuck your lying ass,' was keyed into my hood. Several thousand dollars' worth of damage was done to my truck. "Okay, hold up...Give her ya address, Elaine," I handed Elaine my cell so she could give the 9-1-1 operator her address. As she did, nosey neighbors started coming out of their homes to speculate.

"Here." Elaine gave me back my cell.

"What she say?"

"The police are on their way."

"Welp, I guess our date is off."

"Aw, are you serious, Keelan?"

"Hell yeah. It's gon' take me ah minute to deal with this. Then I have to go to the bank. Shit! And I gotta get ah rental and meet with my pastor. This couldn't have happened at a worse time."

82

"You wanna take my car," Elaine asked. Guilt was beginning to set in.

"Nah, I'ma get ah rental...Damn man, let me call my bro."

Elaine walked around my truck observing it with her arms crossed, "Who you think did this, one of ya li'l girlfriends, evidently."

"Shit, I don't know...Hey bra, I have a situation. Somebody fucked my truck up...I need you to come get me."

Chapter 6

GIVE ME RIGHTEOUSNESS

Five minutes to eleven, I pulled into the driveway of 228 Old Mill Road in Fox Chapel, Pennsylvania. It was a stunning provincial that sat on four acres. The home was a marvel of God's blessing to one of his faithful servants, Pastor Pops Thomas. It's original architectural design blended with modern luxuries, impeccable craftsmanship including beam ceilings, original hardwood flooring, beautiful murals, gourmet kitchen, great room with fireplace, tennis court and in ground pool with cabana. The land even bared a Thomas F. Burke Birdhouse.

Parking my SRX Crossover rental, I looked over the $131,000 S-Class Mercedes Benz that sat out front.

"Brother Keelan," the Pastor called out from his doorway.

"God is good. How's it goin', Pastor?" I asked walking up to him with my hand extended.

"God is great, Brother Keelan. God is great!" Pastor Thomas replied. "Come on in," he added leading the way after shaking my hand.

The inside of Pastor's home was even more revealing of God's favor. I didn't want to offend him by asking the cost of the six bedroom, six and half bath mansion, but through my curiosity I would find out.

"So, you had ah little car problem, huh?"

"Yeeaah yup, a couple of my window's got busted, and the hood got keyed."

"Any ideal of who did it?" Pastor asked.

"Not ah clue, but the police said that a neighbor had wrote down the license plate of a woman seen leaving the scene."

"I've been there," Pastor made a little speech, leading me into the great room. "Straight up."

Hearing Pastor say that surprised me.

"I've had woman issues, I've been locked up numerous times, I was an addict, and that led me to being homeless. I've been through it all."

Inside of the great room were African sculptures, an eighteen-hundred landscape and portrait, a fireplace and bookcases inlaid with bronze fretwork, and two leather club chairs covered in Chatoyant silk.

"Have a seat," Pastor told me after a brief moment of silence. Then for several minutes after there was complete silence as he checked his smartphone. During our introduction he had missed a few calls that needed attended to. I waited patiently for the man of God to address me. Then he placed a call. By the context of his conversation I could tell it was his wife asking him questions. Hearing his answers, I could tell that they were discussing grilled foods.

Listening to his raspy voice, I heard him end his call, and finally he addressed me with a whisper. "Let us stand and pray, Brother Keelan," Pastor said, holding his hands out.

As I stood, we clasped hands, and bowed our heads. Before he started praying, I slightly trembled. Feeling impatient, I waited for the man of God to start praying. I knew that Jesus was with us because the Bible teaches us that, 'When two or more are gathered, he is amongst us'. Jesus also says, 'When two agree concerning anything we ask God for the Father will do it,' in

Matthew 18:19-20. Before another second could elapse he began to pray in Spirit.

"O lord our God, how great you are! You are robed with honor and majesty. You are dressed in a robe of light. Let all that we are praise Jehovah, the Father, and his only begotten Son. The Word, Christ Jesus, Christos Yeshua. Father give righteousness and justice to all who are treated unfairly. Forgive us our sins, and heal all of our diseases. Redeem us from death and crown us with love and tender mercies. Fill our lives with good-things. Renew our youth like the eagles. Let us shone in the prosperity of your chosen ones and never fail you. Amen."

"Amen," I simultaneously said. Opening my eyes, I gave the Pastor a firm handshake then I lifted my head.

"Have a seat, Brother Keelan, what's going on?"

"Pastor, I've sinned in thought and actions. I'm constantly tempted, and I'm being overpowered by the devil and his ways."

"And this about sinful deeds pertaining to what? Jealousy, anger..."

"Women and lust," I answered.

"Oh, I see," Pastor said with a grunt. "Your temptation is getting the best of you, huh, brother? You're succumbing to sensual behaviors, huh?"

"Yes." Shifting in my seat I began to feel discomfort. It started feeling like I was in the hot seat as I revealed the sinner inside of me, and the plying of Pastor's questions was raising the heat by the second.

"Have you committed these sins alone or with a companion or multiple partners?"

I couldn't believe that Pastor was asking me if I masturbated or had sex with multiple women. But the truth was I was doing all of the above. "I'm guilty of it all, Pastor," I truthfully answered.

"And your relationship with your wife?"

"Ex-wife!" I corrected Pastor.

"I thought you two may have worked things out. Marriage is for better or worse. It's been a while since the divorce. When I married you two I believed in you two. I believed that y'all would make it. Have you given up, Brother Keelan? Payton's a good woman."

"Just not the good woman for me, Pastor," I responded.

"Any kids involved?"

His questions reminded me of how little we knew each other. Yes, he did marry us, but that didn't grant our union any special attention. "Nah, but some family members and friends act like they're our kids."

"Oh, they suffer from false guilt, huh?"

"Ha, yeah, they do."

88

"You know God married the first human couple, and even they had problems," the Pastor said, and paused, awaiting my reply.

I shook my head up and down acknowledging what he was saying was true. "Yeah, that is true."

"Are you familiar with the scripture Hebrews 13:4?"

"Let marriage be honorable among all, and the marriage bed be without defilement, for God will judge fornication and adulterers."

"Ha ha ha, right, brother! So you are familiar with scripture?"

"Somewhat. I've searched God's word for answers about my marriage."

"So what made you two get divorced? I ask this because normally, it's the last option when you truly love each other. Meaning, we don't just conclude with divorce without trying to restore the marriage."

"Yeah, we did try to fix our marriage, but we were both unhappy. We could no longer find each other to help one another."

"Mmm, that's deep. But what was the core of the divorce?"

"I called myself surprising her one day. She was out of town on business, and I flew to the city her business meeting was in to be with her."

"And you caught her cheating?"

"Basically. Waiting in the hotel parking lot I saw her and her assistant pull up. First, they were just laughing and joking. I guess they were drunk, you know, feelin' it. And I was just watching. Then they kissed, and I'm like, daaamn!"

"Hold up, brother. This assistant was ah male...Or female?"

"Female."

"Daaamn! Mm...um...mm...Ah...ah."

"Ha...ha...ha, it's cool, Pastor."

The pastor sat up in her chair. "Then what?"

"I got out the car and confronted them."

"What did your wife say?"

"She tried to convince me to be a part, you know?"

"Wow, and you..."

"Just couldn't. I felt betrayed."

"But when I asked you earlier you said you were having threesomes. What was the difference here?"

"She hid this relationship behind my back. I didn't even know my wife was into women."

"Okay, I understand. But y'all tried to patch things up after that, right?"

"Yeah. I tried to make her fire her assistant, but when she refused to, I took it as blatant disrespect."

"That thing must of been real good," Pastor thought, looking at me crazy. "Have you found it in your heart to forgive her. I ain't talking about you just saying you forgive her. I'm talking about you truly forgiving her," Pastor asked.

"I don't think I have, Pastor."

"You know Jesus even forgave Judas, and that was the ultimate betrayal."

"Yeah, I know."

"Matthew 6:15 says, 'If we refuse to forgive others, the Father will not forgive our sins'."

"No, I never read that. Where did you say that was at?"

"Matthew 6:15."

"Oh, Okay...But um, I did forgive her at first, and this little incident had brought us closer, but when she refused to let her assistant go..."

"You refused to forgive her."

"I guess, yup. After that, we would just argue and argue over dumb stuff. It was like we were just causing a situation that was leading to a divorce. We both knew it was over, but neither of us wanted to ask for it, at first."

"Alright, so what can I help you with, specifically."

"The divorce, my loneliness, my sexual addiction...How can I become a good man for a good woman?"

"Well, when Jehovah united Adam and Eve in wedlock, he made no provision for divorce," Pastor Thomas reminded me.

"The word tells us, 'What God has yoked together let no man put apart', in Matthew 19:6, but he also allowed Moses to prescribe divorce as a concession to hard hearts. So there's no sin in getting divorced."

"Correct." Pastor agreed.

"The sin lies in fornication, the adulterers, the anger and so on. And that's what I'm trying to grow through, the divorce and all of the ill effects of it," I continued.

"To get through your bitterness and affliction, 1 Corinthians 4:8-9 kind of explains what you're going through, but it also points out how God is restoring you as you go through these things. It says, 'You're afflicted in every way, but not crushed; perplexed, but not despairing; persecuted, but not forsaken; struck down, but not destroyed. The word of God that is inside of your heart

92

wants you to seek out righteousness. You have to use the good that God has stored inside of you to fight

your outer self, your flesh. But every time you have sex with someone you are not willing to commit to, you are rejecting the Spirit and choosing to do the will of the flesh. You are temporarily pleasing yourself, and you are hurting these women by giving them false hope, Brother Keelan."

"Aw man, Pastor," I expressed as tears streamed down my face.

"The reason your car windows were shattered is because you shattered someone's sense of hope in you."

"Wow!"

"When you commit to these fallacious acts you hurt these women and you put yourself in a position to be punished by God, especially when you cause other members of the church to stumble."

I listened wiping the tears from my face. I studied Pastor's eyes when he made the statement about causing members of the church to stumble. He was telling me that he knew about my relations with the women of the church.

"Psalms 34:18 tells us that God is close to the broken hearted and serves those who are crushed in spirit. So here's where you want to be at, in the position of the broken heart so God can come to your aid. Not in the position in which God will punish you. If you're dealing with heartbreak, be still and let God restore you. Don't go around hurting his children because if you do he will punish you. Matthew 18:6 says that anyone that causes God's little ones who trust in him to stumble and fall into sin, will face punishment that's worse than drowning in the depth of the sea with a large millstone tied around their neck."

"Mm…mm…mm…" No wonder I was so depressed and lonely. I'm wore out from fighting God's discipline.

"Here's what I'm going to do for you, Brother Keelan, I'm going to write down some things that will help you become this good man you speak about," Pastor said, jotting down some things for me on a legal notepad. After several minutes he read them aloud to me. "Alright Brother Keelan, these seven characteristics will give you moral authority, and will embed a discipline that will help to transform you into a good man. Alright here we go. Self-Discipline: In 2 Timothy 1:7, it tells us that God has not given us a spirit of fear and timidity, but power, love, and self-discipline, and you have to use self-discipline to avoid that which causes you to stumble. Your eyes are full of lust, brother. Also check out Matthew 5:27-30, it says,

'Anyone who even looks at a woman with lust has already committed a sin with her heart.' Figuratively speaking, if your eye causes you to lust, gouge it out. Meaning, get rid of bad habits that will bring judgement. Matthew 6:22-23, teaches us that the eye is a lamp that provides light to the body. When your eye is good, your whole body is filled with light, but if your eye is bad, your whole body is filled with darkness. Romans chapter 12, tells us not to copy the behavior and customs of this world, but let God transform us into a new person by changing the way we think so we can become the living and holy sacrifice that he finds acceptable. Verses 9-13, tells us that we must not pretend to love others, but really love them. Hate what is wrong. Hold tightly to what is good. We must love each other with genuine affection, and take delight in honoring each other. Never be lazy, but work hard and serve God enthusiastically. Rejoice in your confident hope. Be patient in trouble, and keep on praying."

"So pastor, the key to my self-discipline is whatever the eye is focused on, whatever I'm focused on?"

"Riiight, right, right! Psalm 119:37 tells us to turn our eyes from worthless things. And study 1 Corinthians 5, it gets deep into church discipline. You can basically use this chapter as a reminder of things and the kind of people to avoid. This chapter will help build your self-discipline. Self-control: 1 Timothy 3 will help you with self-control. The chapter starts off speaking about someone that aspires to be an elder. I want you to put yourself in that position. Verse 2 says, 'We must be men whose lives are above reproach. We must be faithful to our wives.' Now, I know that you are divorced, but here's what I need you to do. Out of all the woman you are involved with, I want

you to pick one woman, and try to be faithful to her for...Let's say, thirty days. Just see how that works for you. But at the same time practice these seven character developments. Okay, so in 1 Timothy 3 it talks about exercising self-control, living wisely, and having a good reputation. Number three is Integrity. Proverbs 10:9 and 20:7 tells us that people with integrity walk safely, blessed are their children who follow them. Remain godly, hate what is false, commit all work to the lord, use words with restraint, being even tempered, acquire God's wisdom and cherish his understanding, gain humility and fear of God. Be willing to confess and forsake sin; and like Job, you will become a man of integrity. Veracity, you must be an open book, Brother Keelan. Allow your partner to look inside of you, and learn your story. Ephesians 4 speaks of a people hopeless and confused. It says their minds are full of darkness, they wander far from the life God gives because they have closed minds and hardened hearts. It tells us to let the spirit renew our thoughts and attitudes. To stop telling lies. To tell our neighbors the truth, and not to sin by letting anger control us. Respect is the next one. For respect, study Titus 2. It's about the right teachings, that promote the kind of living that reflects wholesome teaching. It talks about exercising self-control, being worthy of respect, and living wisely. Brother, make yourself worthy of being respected, and at the time, make sure the woman you chose to be with is worthy of your respect. Next is Valor. As you work on mastering all of these things it will seem as though you are in a fight, and you will be. You will be in a fight against Satan and all of his demons. They will try to tempt you. At times you will fall to temptation and you will sin, but never give up. Call on God through prayer, and he will help you. Keep 1 Corinthians 10:12-13 close at heart, it says, 'If you think you are standing strong, be careful not to fall'. The temptations in your life are no different from what others experience. And God is faithful. He will not allow the temptation to be more than you can endure."

I was familiar with the scriptures 1 Corinthians 10: 12-13.

"When you are tempted, he will show you a way out so that you can endure," we simultaneously recited the end of verse thirteen.

"Yes! So be brave and courageous, Brother Keelan. Phillipians 1:28 tells us not to be intimidated in any way by our enemies. This will be a sign to them that they are going to be destroyed, and you are going to be saved by God himself, and finally, Love. For love, keep Romans 13:8-14 in your heart. We have an obligation to love one another. Love fulfills the requirements of God's law. Remember love does no wrong to others. Brother Keelan, every scripture that I've shared with you is written down on this pad." Pastor handed me the notepad. "If you truly want to be this good man you speak about you will take God's word seriously. You will do as they command you to do and not just listen to them, Brother, you have to obey them in order for them to be effective."

"I got you, Pastor," I said, checking the time on my Longiness wrist-watch. I was surprised to see that two hours had passed. It seemed as if I was only there for a short moment.

"Alright, Brother Keelan, let's stand in prayer."

I sat the notepad down, held Pastor's hands, and bowed my head again for the closing prayer.

"Um-um, Father, we come to you in full expectation of hope that Brother Keelan will conduct himself in a manner worthy of the Good News about Christ Jesus. I pray that his female partner will stand with him in one spirit and purpose, fighting together for faith, which is the Good News.

I pray that you make them truly happy by agreeing wholeheartedly with each other, loving one another, and working together with one mind and purpose. I pray that they don't look out only for their own interest, but they take an interest in each other, too. I pray that they don't let sin control the way they live. I pray that they don't give in to sinful desires, that they don't let any part of their bodies become instruments of evil to serve sin. Instead, give themselves completely to God, and that they use their bodies as instruments to do what is right for the glory of God. Amen! How you feel, Brother Keelan?" Pastor asked after praying.

"Like I was dead, but now I have new life."

Chapter 7

LORD, SAVE US ALL

"Itch, um! Itch, um! Itch, um!" The pointed end of On deck's shovel piercing through the semi-hard surface of the earth was the only thing you could hear echoing throughout the wooded area.

On Deck had buried a large sum of cash, and concentrated on getting to it. Dig after dig he anxiously waited to hear the sound of metal hitting metal, and not just shovel striking dirt. It was the second ditch he had dug. He knew that his hidden treasure was there somewhere waiting beneath the turf. The tree he had buried it near was a distinguishing one from the others. Besides that, he had carved the initials B.P. on the side of the tree it was buried on. What he couldn't remember was if it was buried five-feet or ten from the base of the large tree. Occasionally, he would look back at the initials. B.P.

stood for: The Big Payback and he planned on doing just that, pay back everyone that had done him wrong or left him for dead.

During his incarceration several of his little hordes had come up, but now that he was home most of them were crying about how high the coke prices were, and how messed up the game was. But he wasn't trying to hear any of that. He had put some money up and planned on putting it to good use.

"Come on! I know ya here, baby. Come on!"

"Itch, um! Dink! Dink! Dink! Dink! DINK!"

"Yes!" He said, finally unearthing his riches.

On his knees, he blocked out the freezing sensation of coldness that made his fingers feel as though they were burning, as he dug around the two metal safety boxes that held seventy-five thousand dollars in each one of them. Clearing the border around the two boxes that sat side by side. He tried to pull them from their frigid, slushy-like grave. The weather had been in the thirties all week, but on this particular day, it had reached a high of sixty-four degrees, causing the snow covered dirt to become cold and muddy. On Deck couldn't wait any longer to retrieve his money. He had kept his eyes on the weather since his release waiting for such an opportunity, and when he saw how nice it was going to be that day, he grinned ear to ear.

"Grrr-ah! Grrr-aaah! Grrr-ah," the long underground stay of the safety-boxes, along with the weather, helped the boxes resist his pulls and tugs. Getting frustrated and impatient, On Deck, used his shovel to pry the portable vaults from the grounds frosty grasp.

After finally pulling the boxes from their muddy burial, he looked over the two noncombustible safes and was pleased to see that they were still intact. Placing them in a large, black duffle bag, he hoisted it over his back, landing it on the edge of his right shoulder and exited the timbered dwellings, leaving behind the shovel and three holes in the terrene surface of the woods. Wiping his muddy hands on his green Dickie pants, he pulled out his car key, and popped the trunk. After putting the bag inside of it, he closed it, walked around to the driver's door, unlocked it and got in before pulling off. He dialed his little homie's cell phone number. After a few rings, the young hustler answered.

"What up, big homie?"

"You put that together fo' me?" On Deck asked him.

"I'm trying to now, big homie. Give me ah day or so."

"Cool, hit me when you get it together."

"Got you." The little homie said.

On Deck, hung up, and called another baller, but got no answer. As he went to place his phone in the hole of his cup holder, it buzzed.

"Yo Concrete, what up, homie?"

"Shit. Chilling. What's up?" Concrete said in a slumbered tone.

"Hm…You ah…Put that together fo' me?"

"Maaan, I told you it was fucked up out here. I ain't got no five stacks to give you, dawg!"

"Nigga, rna'fuckas told me how ya ass is ballin' out here, poppin' bottles, buying property an' shit. Nigga, you drive ah Aston…"

"There you go counting my money, all in my pockets. I told you I got you, but you gotta wait, right now."

The phone line got quiet for a moment.

"Hello?!" Concrete thought On Deck had hung up on him.

"Yeah, I'm here. Look, the least you could do is throw me ah stack, to hold me until you get the rest."

"Until I get the rest, huh?" Concrete sarcastically repeated. "I'm not no young boy no more, dawg." He thought to himself. "Alright, stop over in like an hour," Concrete told On Deck.

"Good look, I'll be there in ah hour." On Deck didn't like Concrete's energy. He didn't like him coming at him with all that tough-shit. He had put him in the game, and now Concrete was

acting funny. He had asked two of his little homies for five stacks a piece, but neither one of them had come through for him that's why he had to borrow money from his brother. Now he could pay his brother back, and take care of some things he needed to take care of. Whenever his little homies came through that would just be bonus money.

Hanging up from his call with Concrete, On Deck then dialed his B.M.'s number. "Concrete? Nigga, you ain't solid. I'll bust through ya shit, boy!" On Deck said to himself. Not feeling the conversation, he had with his young homie.

"Hello?!" Belleza Greene, On Deck's baby mama, answered.

"Yo?! What you doin', Bella?" On Deck asked.

"Waiting for your daughter to get out of the tub so she can get dressed, and we can get outta here."

"Where y'all goin'?"

104

"I don't know, somewhere."

"I'm tryna...You know...Get it in."

"You should be cool after last night, Deck."

On Deck wanted to have sex, but they had sex the night before, and Bella felt as if that was enough, at least until later.

"I'm backed up. I've been gon' fo' years. I'm tryna unload in yo mouth, ass..."

"Not now, your daughter ain't having it. Plus, my son's about to wake up."

"Ya son, huh?"

"Yes, my son, Deck."

On Deck restrained from saying anything about her son. "Where his sucka ass dad at? I ain't seen his ass yet, but when I do..."

"Stop it, Deck!"

"You right. Look, I'll be there in like ten minutes."

"Okay," Bella said before hanging up. "We gotta hurry up, Deck is on his way back," she told her other baby daddy, Lamar.

Lamar and On Deck had grew up together, but had fell out because Lamar had got Bella pregnant. He tried to apologize to On Deck before he came home, but On Deck had hung up on him.

After Bella sat her phone down, Lamar nodded his head downward, indicating that he wanted some head. Placing his hand behind Bella's head, he pulled it towards his crouch. Bella took him in, and pleasured him until he released his load into her mouth. Bella tried to pull her head back, but Lamar held it down until he finished cumming.

"Pah-pah-pah, ugghh...Why you do that, Lamar?! I told you not to cum in my mouth," Bella said spitting semen into her hand.

Lamar laughed as he stood zipping his pants up, "Let me get outta here 'fa' this fool get here. I ain't messing with that boy."

"You want me to wake ya son up, so he can see you before you leave?" Bella asked walking into the kitchen to rinse her mouth out in the kitchen sink.

"Naw, he the reason I'm in trouble now. If you would have got that abortion I wouldn't be going through it with Deck."

"WHAT?! Bye, Lamar! What the hell is you talkin' 'bout?"

"Alright, I'll hit you later."

"Leave us some money," Bella told Lamar walking back into the living room.

"Hm, here go fifty, I'll give you more later on."

"Quit playing, nigga. What is this, McDonald's money?"

Lamar pulled his bailer knot back out, and pulled off five twenty dollar bills."

"See, that's a shame. Look at all that money you got, and you gon' give us fifty-dollars? That's crazy. I'm taking care of our son, and ya ass is being tight."

"I gotta flip, this flip money. I told you I got you later," Lamar said pecking Bella on the lips. "Here, I'm out."

"Yeah, whatever. I still want more later."

"I got you."

Fifteen minutes later, On Deck pulled up and parked in front of Bella's. Bella watched On Deck get out of the car and go to the trunk. After a few minutes, he closed it, and walked towards the house with his money in a white grocery bag.

"Here comes ya daddy, Dor'," she told her daughter, getting her son, Lamar Jr. dressed.

"Daddy...Daddy...Daddy," Doraine yelled running down the steps to greet her father.

"Hey, princess." On Deck hugged his daughter with his bag of money in his hand.

"Did you buy me something, daddy?" Doraine asked hugging on her dad with the bag in his hand in mind.

"You want daddy to buy you something? What you want, baby?"

Doraine let her dad go and looked at him thinking about what she wanted. "I don't know, daddy. I want to go to the store and see."

"Okay."

"Mm, daddy..."

"Yes, Dori."

"Why you all dirty? You need to take a bath like me."

On Deck laughed going into the living room where he took a seat on the couch. Bella and Lamar Jr. were on their way downstairs. Looking around the living room for the TV remote, On Deck noticed something and looked closely at it. He believed it to be a drop of semen on the dark colored couch. "What the fuck is that?!"

"What?" Bella asked walking into the living room. Seeing On Deck on the couch her and Big Lamar was on made her heart pound harder and harder.

"Dor', go upstairs..."

"Aw, daddy!"

"Doraine! Go upstairs!"

Bella looked at what On Deck was talking about. "O-M-G! How could I slip like this?" Bella questioned herself. "I don't know what that is." She played dumb.

"Bitch, don't try to play me!" On Deck stood up and yelled. "You know..."

"BITCH?! I'm not ya bitch...Lamar, go upstairs with ya sister," Bella ordered her son to go upstairs.

"Mmmm-whhyyy..." Lamar Jr. started crying.

"Boy, shut up, and go upstairs!" Bella said to her son.

"So, who was it? His dad? You still fuckin' that nigga?!" On Deck asked, walking closer to Bella.

"Get out my face, Deck. I'm tellin' you!" Bella avoided the question. Inside she was scared as hell. She knew how violent On Deck could get, but she stood her ground.

"You know what, I'm out!"

"How you leaving? You ain't taking my car!"

"Bitch! That's my car!"

"You take my car, and ya ass'll be in jail."

On Deck just looked at Bella. He wanted to beat her ass, but he had too much money on him. Then his phone buzzed. After digging into his pocket, he answered it. Walking away from the argument.

"Yo?!"

"We about to pull up." The caller on the line told On Deck.

"Cool. I'll be at the spot, meet me there."

Click! The line went dead.

Going to the bag that sat on the couch, he looked over at Bella. Her arms were crossed, and her face was balled up. The kids were on the steps.

"Dor', come here," On Deck told his daughter, digging into the bag. He made sure all of the bundles of cash were still there then he dug into his pocket, and pulled out a large wad of money. Peeling off a few hundred, he gave it to his daughter. "Mommy's gon' take you to the store..."

"You not coming, daddy?"

"Not this time, baby. Daddy..."

"Where you get all that money from, Deck?" Bella cut On Deck off.

"Don't worry 'bout it! Look baby, I'll come get you tomorrow," On Deck said to his daughter, looking at Lamar Jr holding his big sister's hand. "You want some money too, lil man?"

"Mm-hm," Lamar Jr gestured sticking his little hand out, "I want some candy."

"You want some candy, huh, lil man?"

110

"I want some money too," Bella stuck her hand out.

"You was just about to call the law on me. Now you want some money," On Deck pulled a few hundred off and gave them to Lamar Jr. "Go buy you a lot of candy, and some new J's, lil man," On Deck said to Lamar Jr.

Lamar Jr. smiled at On Deck. "Wank you, Deck."

"You welcome, lil man." Then On Deck, pulled off ten more hundred dollar bills, and gave them to Bella. "Fuckin' cheatin' ass rat."

"Daddy?!" On Deck's daughter didn't like him calling her mother names. "Be nice, daddy," she told him.

On Deck smiled and gave his daughter a kiss. "Come on y'all, let's go to the store."

"Yaaay!" The kids got excited.

"Go get y'all's coats. Thanks, Deck," Bella said switching her fat ass side to side, walking away. "Hurry up, y'all!"

Chapter 8

CHANGE IS GON' COME

"POLICE!" Four narcotics officers kicked in Concrete's front door. "GET DOWN! GET DOWN!"

Concrete did as he was told and slowly got down on the floor as did his girlfriend. They were sitting in their living room, smoking weed, when the police busted into their house.

"IS THERE ANYBODY ELSE HERE?!"

"My three kids are upstairs," Concrete's girlfriend told the officer.

"CLEAR!" One officer called out from upstairs in the apartment. "We have three small children up here."

"I'm sending their mother up. Get up, and go upstairs with your kids." The officer told Concrete's girlfriend. "I'm sending the mom up. Come here," the officer told Concrete's girlfriend to come to him, and he searched her

112

for drugs and weapons. "What's this? Pull it out," he felt something in her back pocket. It was a bag of weed. She pulled it out and showed the officer.

"Throw it on the table, and get ya ass upstairs! You should be ashamed of yourself. Three kids, on drugs, selling drugs, get ya stankin' ass upstairs fo' it be some police brutality going on in this bitch. GET UPSTAIRS! And just know I'm taking ya ass to jail, too. Damn kids don't need to be with no drug using, drug dealing ass momma! And you, you sorry diaper of smelly, crack baby shit, GET UP! GET UP! And do it slowly. I'm looking fo' ah reason to take you outta this world cause it's low life dudes like you that just keep fuckin' it up, and fuckin' it up!"

"Got something!" One of the officers yelled out from the kitchen.

"That's ya ass," the leading officer told Concrete. "What you got some druuugggs..." The officer, tauntingly asked his fellow officer.

"Nah, some money."

"I got some drugs," the other officer searching the kitchen said.

"That's ya ass, boy!"

113

"Whatever!" Concrete said putting his head down in disgrace.

"What you say?!"

Concrete didn't repeat himself. He just sat there, mad at himself because he had been telling himself that he was going to take his money over to his mom's house.

"Whoa! Where you get this?" The leading officer asked his fellow officer. "Mm, let me guess, the freezer?" The bundles of money were cold. "How much is this?"

Concrete didn't say anything.

"I asked you a question," the leading officer stated, stepping to Concrete.

Concrete looked up. "Forty-stacks."

The officer that found the drugs walked up to the living room table and dumped two boxes of cereal out on it. Cereal and bricks of dope poured onto the table.

"OH MY DOPE DEALERS! Boy, ya ass is in trouble now." The leading officer said.

"Found some more money. This boy got ah Chip A'Hoy cookie bag full of hundreds!" The officer that found the money in the freezer yelled to the other officers.

"Whaaat?! Not a bag full of hundreds."

"Did you search him," the officer that found the drugs in the cereal boxes asked.

114

"Not yet." The leading officer answered.

"Stand up." The officer told Concrete.

Concrete stood up. "I gotta gun on me." Concrete said in a low tone of voice.

"What you say," the leading officer asked, walking closer to Concrete.

"I gotta gun on me," he repeated himself.

"GUN! GUN! GUN!" The fellow officer yelled.

The officer upstairs with Concrete's girlfriend and kids drew his weapon, and pointed it at his girlfriend. His children started screaming and crying.

"Don't kill my mommy...No! Don't kill my mommy..."

The officer searching the kitchen pulled out his gun and ran into the living room. When he got in there he saw the leading officer take Concrete's gat, and hit him over the head with it. BOP!

"You try'na kill me, huh. You was try'na kill me!"

Bop! Bop! Bop! Bop!" He pistol-whipped Concrete.

"What's going on down there?!" The officer upstairs yelled out.

"Everything's clear down here." One of the fellow officers yelled back.

"Okay, alright. I'm not going to kill ya mother. Calm down, calm down."

"Aaagh agh, stop! Please stop! I wasn't try'na kill you!" Concrete pleaded with the leading officer.

Out of breath, the leading officer stopped pistol-whipping Concrete. The other officer stood back and watched. "You know what we should do, fellas?" The leading officer asked.

"What's that? Nah, what?" The officers asked.

"We should kill his ass. Say he pulled his gun on me, and take it all."

"Please don't! Take it all. Just don't kill me. I got kids, man." Concrete begged for his life.

The officer looked over at him. "Okay, you got two choices..."

Buzzzz...Nnnnn...Buzzzz...Nnnn! Concrete's phone started vibrating.

One of the fellow officers looked at the screen display. "Deck?! Who's Deck, he ya connect?" The officer asked.

"Nawl, he's just my homie. He just came home. He ain't doing nothing," Concrete told the officers.

They all looked at each other. The officer with the phone answered it. "Hello Deck...He's with us, the police right now. I hope you ain't try'na buy no drugs cause he's gonna be all out when we get done with him!"

CLICK!

"Hello...Hello! I think ya friend hung up," the officer said looking at the phone. "Yup, he did."

Concrete just shook his head. He knew he was done. That phone call really did it for him. If the 'hood heard about that phone call, he knew that he could be dead within the next twenty-four hours.

"Man, what you try'na do, get me killed?!" Concrete asked.

"Now, like I was saying, you got two choices. You can go to jail, and we tell all ya homies that you told on them..."

"WHAT?! You're crazy!" Concrete said.

"Or you can stop wasting our time, take me to all of your stashes, and we can be outta here in say, ten minutes. Depending on how fast you do it. But if I think ya bullshitting us, the deals off the table. Now what you gonna do?" The leading officer asked.

"If I give everything to y'all, I'm good, I won't go to jail?" Concrete asked seeing a little light at the end of the dark tunnel he was in. The police were making his life a living hell.

"Correct! We let you go. But you can't bullshit us..."

"I'm not! Come on, yawl got most of it. I got like twenty stacks and two ki's upstairs..."

"TWO KILOS?! I don't know..."

"Come on, man! You said you would let me go."

"It's ya lucky day." The leading officer said.

"It don't feel like it," Concrete said leading the police to the last of his stash.

"Look at it this way, you could be spending the rest of ya life in jail, but you'll be back on ya feet in ah hour."

After the narcotics officers got all of the drugs, guns, and money in Concrete's house, they made Concrete and his girlfriend lay face down on the living room floor. "Don't get up until ten minutes after we're gone. If I see one of y'all come to the door as we're pulling off, we're gonna come back in here, and take y'all asses to jail!"

After ten minutes went by, Concrete got his phone, and called On Deck back. "Deck, man, look, mafuckas took everything I had here...Nah, I told them you just came home, and wasn't doing nothing, I know...But look, 'member that five-stacks you wanted I'll give you ten if you keep that little phone call between us...Nah, I ain't no rat! They just took eh'thang, and let me go."

***

Fifteen minutes later, the narcotics officers that had took Concrete's drugs, guns, and money, pulled up in front of the house On Deck was paroled to. But they wouldn't be kicking in his door, yelling at him, or taking anything from him. They didn't even have their Pittsburgh Task Force windbreakers on. The leading officer knocked on On Deck's front door.

"Yo?! Come on in, y'all." On Deck let the narcotics officers in. "How did things go?" On Deck asked.

"Shit was sweet as ah mother, dawg." The leading officer said.

"I see y'all brought me a big Santa bag. I hope it's a lot of money in that bag," On Deck playfully said.

"It is," one of the fellow officers said, pouring the contents of the bag out on the floor.

"MERRR-EEEE CHIST-MAS!" On Deck screamed.

On Deck, and the fake narcotics officers laughed. The four officers weren't officers at all, they were friends of Fishscale, On Deck's ex-bunky.

After the way Concrete had talked to On Deck on the phone, he called them, and put them on to the lick. Now they were all thousands of dollars richer, and because On Deck used Fishscale's homies he would make sure that they all gave him a cut of their share of the drugs and money.

Chapter 9

DATE NIGHT

On this warm winter evening, an hour had passed. Teal and I were enjoying each other's company. We continually joked and laughed. And though it had not been worded, she was giving me a seductive vibe with the help of her long mesmerizing stares and inviting smile. Our date was going great.

Bold, beautiful, and successful, she was desirable enough to play a character in a David Weaver novel. For our first date, Teal decided that she wanted to spend it at a Baking Class. My choice for a date was dinner, but I was willing to try this. Nonetheless, I was happy I allowed her to choose our place to meet.

As she giggled, I laughed. Other baking novices eyeballed us and grinned discomforting smiles, but we didn't care. Teal had a carefree spirit, and I loved that about her.

Because of the damage done to my truck earlier that day, our date had started off tense. But sensing something was wrong, Teal eased my tension. "It's gonna be okay. I'm not that bad, Keelan," she told me, breaking the ice.

Hearing her sensual sounding voice calmed my nerves and cracked a smile across my face. "My fault, I just gotta couple things on my mind that I need to let go."

"Let 'em go then," Teal said placing her soft hand atop of mine. Her touch made me look her in the eyes. I wondered if the good woman I was looking for was inside of her. "Because I'm not try'na share my time with a good looking man with ah bad attitude," she continued.

"Hm, hm, you don't have to," I assured her. "So what's up with this baking thing? Do you like to bake? Well, of course, you have to. Plus, we're on our way to ah baking class. That was ah dumb question," I said, asking and answering my own question, and then criticizing myself. I felt awkward. I was trying to start up a conversation, but failed at it with a lame attempt.

"No, it wasn't," Teal said rebounding my crack at starting a dialogue.

"Huh?" Still in thought, I was lost by her response.

"Your question, it wasn't a stupid question. Because I can't bake. Well, not the way I want to. I mean I can

122

follow Betty Crocker directions, but I wanna learn how to bake from scratch.

"You do, huh?" I asked with a chuckle.

"Wouldn't you like that? Wouldn't you like me to cook you homemade biscuits?" She asked resting her hand atop of mine again.

"Sure," I said, looking at her again. "So, we're going to be baking biscuits?"

"I don't know, Keelan. I'm just saying," she laughed.

As our engagement went on, I wished I wouldn't have avoided her as much in the past. But then again, if I hadn't, I would have probably called off our appointed time to share together.

Inside of a small studio kitchen, our small group of four couples wrapped our aprons around our bodies and placed our chef hats on our heads. Teal had brought her own bedazzled apron and hat. Her apron read, *#1 Baker*.

"Ghet-toooo!" I whispered with my eyes bulging out of my head in humor. The class, including the instructor, burst out in laughter.

"SHUT UP, KEELAN!" Teal said in embarrassment. Playfully, punching my arm, "Don't be hatin'!"

The class chuckled again.

Looking at our ingredients, I couldn't wait to flour her beautiful golden brown face.

After listening and following every instruction the pastry cook gave us, we all placed our baked goods in the industrial oven and waited as they baked. Waiting, we introduced ourselves to each other. There were two white couples, a Hispanic couple, and us. Chatting amongst ourselves, we barely paid attention to the baking instructor. It was as if we could care less if our snicker doodles came out as instructed, or what the teacher was saying after we placed our bakeries in the oven. The women grouped up with women, and men with men. Laughter made us feel comfortable with each other's company as we waited for our finished product. And then I did it. "POOF!" I flung a small cloud of flour, covering Teal's bedazzled apron with white powdery substance.

"NO YOU DIDN'T!" Teal said looking for a food substance to throw back. When I saw her pick up an egg, I backed away from her, and then she threw it.

"CRACK!" Unable to dodge it, the egg hit me in the head, and yoke ran down my face. Everybody laughed. The next thing I knew, the other couples, and the instructor, participated in the small food fight. Of course, it was men verses the women, and they got the best of us.

I had egg all over me. Then "TINK!" The oven alerted, letting us know that our snicker doodles were done.

Once we were done cooking and cleaning up, we prepared to leave. "Okay, nice to meet you...See y'all next week..." we shook hands with the other couples and said our goodbyes. We all agreed to return to the class the following week. Even the Pastry Baker said that she looked forward to seeing us again and because I started the food fight, I gave her a hundred dollars for cleaning up the mess we made.

"Look at my hair! Uugghhh, I could kill you!" Teal said fingering through her curly locks of long black tresses.

Looking at her flour covered face, I laughed. "That was fun, thanks," I said.

"Whatever! I'm still gonna get you."

"For what?"

"Look at me. I gotta wash my hair, and everything. I should make you wash it."

"No problem," I said without thinking about it.

"So now what?" Teal asked not wanting the night to end. Neither did I. It was only 9:14 pm, and neither one of us had anything else to do.

"I don't know. It's ya call."

"Well, my kids are gone for the weekend." Teal had two boys, a seven, and an eleven-year-old. I had yet to meet them. She was the type of woman that didn't allow men to be around her children unless she was sure that she wanted them around, and I respected that.

"I'll tell you what," Teal started off saying. "Take me to my place so I can gather some things, then we can go to your place and shower, and get dressed for dinner, or maybe ah movie." She continued with a sly smile on her face, but her expression wasn't a sneaky one. It was more seductive.

"Cool, let's do it." I agreed to extending our date, stealing every glance I could possibly get of the highly attractive woman I was sharing my evening with. She was gorgeous in every way, even covered in flour. But a shower...Dinner...A movie? Teal wasn't fooling me, she wanted to have sex just as bad as I did. But I reminded myself of the conversation I had with Pastor Thomas and said a little prayer with a hard-on, hoping it would keep me strong even after a couple of drinks.

After picking up a few things from Teal's house on the Southside of Pittsburgh, we drove to my place. "Here, taste my snicker doodle," Teal said in a childish, whiny voice.

"Mmmm, it's alight," I joked. Actually, it was delicious.

"It's better than yours!"

"Yeah right!" I said, chewing. "Give me another bite," I said, making her laugh.

"I told you mines was better than yours."

"Yeeaah, Okay. Maybe ah little bit."

"Wow! This is where you live at?" Teal asked as we pulled into my building's parking garage.

"Yup," I replied exiting my rental. "Grab' up the snicker doodles, I got ya stuff." I told her.

Walking into my abode, she slowly followed me, inspecting it without seeming obvious. "This is nice."

"Thank you." I thanked Teal, thinking about an article I read one day waiting in my marriage counselor's front lounge. It said that your home is like your clothing, it's a symbol of who you are. It reflects the best you.

"Echo, Evening Playlist," I commanded my Amazon Echo to play something smooth, and the Isley Brothers', *For The Love of You*, began to play.

"Uh-uh," Teal expressed her non-approval. "I need something to turn up to. What you got to sip on?" She asked.

"You want ah MYX?"

"That's Nicki Minaj's new Moscato, right?"

"Yup."

"Yeah, that'll do."

"Echo, turn up!" I commanded and Dabb Lord by local artist, Asco, started blaring from its speaker.

"That's what I'm talking about," Teal said.

I walked into my bedroom, and handed her a bottled Moscato.

After taking a few sips of her drink, Teal, wasted no time getting undressed. Her body was flawless. 'Bycycle' exercises defined her stomach, her waist was 22 inches, her eyes were hazel-brown, and her skin tone was slightly a shade darker.

"You coming? You said you were going to wash my hair, come on," she said, asking if I was going to take a shower with her.

"Uh-uh, go 'head. I'll get in after you." I was trying to fight temptation. Again, Pastor's voice was sounding in my head. "Just enjoy her company. No sex!" I told myself as my penis whined

like a hurt puppy. Just walking away without further discussion, Teal didn't seem phased by me not joining her. It was as if she was telling me that it was my lost, and not hers.

"Where are we going to eat? Have you figured out, yet?" Teal asked, calling out from the shower.

"You want to go to the Savoy?" I asked, raising my voice so she could hear me over the running water in the shower. Then in a split-second, I had changed my mind, took off my clothes, and went to join Teal in the shower stall. Sliding back the shower curtain, Teal briefly gazed at my long extended phallus.

"Hello," she said. But I didn't know if she was addressing me or it. By looking at the angle of her face I could tell that she was pleased either way.

After thoroughly examining my physic, she handed me a bottle of shampoo. It was as if she knew that I would change my mind.

As I helped Teal wash her hair, we held a small conversation about our professional careers. She told me that she had read my article on my Blog and liked it. And I complimented her independence. Before I knew it, her hair was rinsed out, and she was exiting the shower stall. After washing up, I did the same.

Fresh out of the shower, I bobbed my head to Owey's *Whoa*, as it played on my Echo. As I wiped off the warm beads of water that rolled down my Atlas frame, I recited the late trap rapper Bankroll Fresh's verse. Owey had collaborated with him and Young Dolph on the song.

Smiling, I was proud of myself. It was the first time in a long time that I had showered with a woman, and restrained from having sex with her. My dilemma made think of the conversation God had with Cain before he killed his brother. God told Cain, "You will be accepted if you do what is right. But if you refuse to do what is right, then watch out! Sin is crouching at the door, eager to control you. But you must subdue it and be its master."

Wrapping my towel around my waist, I walked into the bedroom, unraveled it, and let it fall to the floor. Lotioning my body, I gave Teal a show that made me feel like a male stripper.

Stunned by the chiseled sculpture of my anatomy, Teal paused with her lipstick suspended a quarter inch away from her mouth. "Mm-mm-mm!" She moaned as her eyes scanned my body up and down. It was her turn to fight temptation.

"What?!" I asked acting dumb with a smile on my face.

"Keelan, you know what!" Teal said rolling her eyes. Turning away from me, she looked in the mirror, and continued to apply her lipstick. Then she paused as if a

130

thought had struck her. After surveilling the room, she grabbed her purse, and dumped its contents onto the bed, exposing her passport, keys, Dolce perfume, a book by rapper turned author Rae Zellous titled, *Pink Widows*, and several other items that she combed through until she found her driver's license. "Got it!" She said.

After slipping on my Tommy Hilfiger briefs, I opened my closet in search of something to wear, and pulled out a black tuxedo-styled jacket by Brunello Gucinelli, then I put on a black T-shirt by Unis, black Pantherella socks, and black shoes by Robert Giergerie to go with it.

"How I look?" Teal asked me. She was dressed in a see through flowered lace top, Python printed stretch pants that hugged her crouch, and complimented her voluptuous derriere, and a shoulder less alligator jacket that cut off right below her breast. Her outfit visualized her animal instincts.

"You look AAAH-MAZINC!!" I told her.

"Mmmuu-aah, thank you, baby," she said with a kiss. "You ready," she asked.

"I am."

"Let's get outta here. I'ma drive us there."

"Oh, you gonna drive?"

"Yeah. I'll drive us there. But you gonna have to drive us back 'cause I already know I'ma be hit."

And there it was in one statement. Not only would we be spending the night together, I would be waking up to a sexy ass breakfast guest too.

Chapter 10

TABLE FOR TWO

Ten minutes from the *Savoy Restaurant*, "I should be there in ah few minutes. Okay. Thanks, my man Chuck reserved a table for us," I told Teal.

'Chuck,' was Chuck Sanders, the CEO of Urban Lending Solutions. A former Pittsburgh Steeler that is credited with launching a program that gives staff members skills to modify troubled mortgages through his company's usual training.

Teal and I made plans to have dinner at the *Savoy Restaurant*, and then they would go to a club afterwards if their night continued to be a pleasurable one. At a stop light they could hear the blaring bass coming from a car behind them, I looked at the driver bobbing his head through his rearview mirror. "You hungry,"

"Mmmhm, ah lil bit. You?" Teal asked.

"Hell yeah."

"Thought you filled up off of my delicious snickerdoodles," Teal jokingly said.

"You wish. They weren't that good, ha...ha...ha. I need some real food," Keelan said laughing at Teal's remark.

"Whatever, Keelan. You know mine were better than yours, ha...ha." Teal said, then paused for a few seconds, "Keelan , can I ask you a question?" She asked.

"Yes, anything. Wassup?"

"Why hasn't your phone rung? Did you turn it off or somethin'? I haven't seen you on it one time tonight, and I know you got women all over you," Teal said.

"Ha...ha, where's your phone? You haven't really been on your either," I answered Teal's question with a question.

"I've been on my phone. I had to check on my kids. But my business phone is off," Teal stated.

"Mines is too. I left it at home. This phone...," I tapped the pocket his phone was in, "is for emergencies only," I told Teal.

"Ha...ha, this one is too," Teal said holding her phone up. "After the baking class I said that I was going to give you as much of my undivided as I could."

134

"That's what's up. I feel the same way. You know I just didn't want the distraction of my phone getting in the way of our connection, you know?"

"Whhaat?! Aw, Keelan, I feel so special.

"No, for real."

"Mhmm, give me a kiss," Teal said puckering her lips up.

Keelan kissed Teal. "I try not to let my phone control my life. I know for some people their life revolves around their phone."

"Mines definitely do. That's why I know you're someone special because I don't turn my phone off for nobody. The last date I went on it was so boring I played ah game on my phone the whole time."

"No, you didn't, Teal?!"

"Oh, yes I did. That was ah date outta hell. All he did was talk about himself, and how successful he was, what he had, and all that."

"Oh, he couldn't detach himself from his belongings. I bet he was on his phone almost as much as you were."

"Yeah, he was. Talking 'bout eh'thang was business. He was on his phone the first thirty-minutes of our date…"

"And that's when you declared phone war, huh?" I said with a chuckle.

"Hell yeah. That nigga wasn't talking business eh' time he answered the phone," Teal laughed thinking about the date. "That reminds of the story in the Bible about the *Rich Young Man*, have you read it?" Keelan asked.

"Yeah. When the guy asked Jesus what he had to do to inherit eternal life?" Teal was familiar with the parable.

"Yup, *Mark 10:17-22*. The young dude was ballin' and indeed righteous. When Jesus told him he had to follow the Commandments, he told Jesus he had been following them since he was young..."

"Then Jesus told him that there was still one thing he didn't do," Teal said.

"Yeah, Jesus said, *go and sell all of ya possessions and give the money to the poor, and you will have treasure in heaven. Then come follow me.* Hearing this the young dude's face fell, and he went away sad. Now just imagine this happening in these days and times. Jesus rollin' up on ah believer that's attached to their phone and says, *look, there's been a change of plans...*"

"Keelan?!" Teal cracked up laughing after hearing my modern day scenario.

"In order for you to get eternal life from me, you gon' hav' tah sell ya phone and give the money to the po'. What would you say?"

"You're funny as hell," Teal giggled.

"What would you say?".

"Hmm, I don't know. I got too much goin' on wit' my phone, and usually I use two phones," Teal said.

"Two phones? That's crazy, though. How you gon' tell Jesus that? So basically, when it comes down to it you gon' pick ya phone over eternal life?"

"Come on, Keelan, fo' real? You try'na say I ain't goin' to have eternal life because of my cell phone? Stop it!" Teal said with a giggle and a smile on her face.

"No! Definitely not, I'm just sayin' you said you got too much goin' on witcha phone, like…" Keelan paused. "Like it would be ah hard choice for you. But I'm most definitely not qualified to say who's going to heaven or hell. or who will have eternal life and who won't. But let me ask you this, though, how many of us in the church do you believe would give up their phones if ever put in that position?"

"Um, ah, I…I don't know. That's ah hard one," Teal said giving Keelan's question deep thought.

"Okay, let me ask you this, would you say our phones are like idols?"

"Mm, maybe. "

"Like ah god to us. Was our cell phones made by the hands of the devil to trick us, to lead us astray from God!" I said in a preacher's tone of voice.

"KEEE-LAN! KEE-LAN! STOP IT! STOP! You crazy!" Teal laughed hysterically.

"I'm tellin' you, Teal, that phone is like a false god to some of us."

"Whoa! Ah god?"

"Well, think about it. Our love for it is the root of all evil. It's just like money. I'm not saying the phone itself is evil, but the love for it leads to a lot of evil, terrorist acts, pornography, social media outlets, and so on and so on. The more we use it, the more we depend on it, the more it controls us."

Teal sat quietly, and listened to Keelan, impressed by how deeply rooted he was in the Word of God.

"We live in a materialistic world where many of us serve what we desire, like our phones. People go crazy when Apple brings out a new phone. We line up for hours or days to get it. Then we spend all of our time on it, textin', gossipin', lustin', shoppin', and judgin'. Our desire for our phones and all that we do with it far outweighs our commitment to God and spiritual matters. The stuff we put on our phones like the apps, the social media pages, all the stuff we store on our phones consumes us. And whatever consumes us we spend much of our time and energy thinking about. That's why I say that the love for our phone is the root of all kinds of evil. If you study 1 Timothy 6:10, you'll understand what I'm talkin' 'bout. Now, let me ask you ah couple more question, then we can go inside, and eat," I said. They had pulled in and parked close to Savoy, and sat in the car talking.

"Go 'head," Teal said listening attentively.

"How many times have you prayed, praised and worshiped this week?"

"Ah couple," Teal answered.

"Did you go to church last week?"

"No."

"Now, how many times were you on ya phone this week?"

"I can't even count. I don't know. All the time, all day, every day," Teal said analyzing the question.

"Then can you honestly say that God, and not ya phone is ya master," I continued.

Teal didn't say a word.

139

"Matthew 6:24 teaches us that no one can serve two masters. It says, *'For you will hate one and love the other; you will be devoted to one and despise the other. You cannot serve God and money'* or ya phone. That's what Jesus was try'na teach the rich young man."

"Okay...Okay, Keelan! You're gettin' too deep for me. You got me wantin' to throw my damn phone away, wonderin' if I'ma be granted eternal life, and you blew my damn buzz wit' all that. You got me thinkin 'bout too much. Can we just go eat?"

"I'm sorry, baby. I didn't mean to get carried away. It's just that when I start talkin' about Jesus, I just go all out. He's been good to me so anytime I get to talk about him I do, I'm sorry."

"No, you ain't gotta be sorry about that," Teal said feeling ashamed about making me feel bad for bringing the Lord and Savior, Jesus Christ up.

"Well, I can say our phones don't control us 'cause we both turned ours off," Keelan started saying.

"Right!" Teal agreed.

"All I gotta do is get you to church," Keelan said smiling at Teal.

"I told you I'll go with you next Sunday," Teal said.

"That's wassup," I said as we unbuckled their seatbelts. "Let me get'cha door," he told Teal.

"Okay. You're such ah gentleman, Keelan," Teal said, giving her make up one last check in the visor mirror. When she looked up, she was greeted by me opening her door.

"Thank you, Keelan," Teal said.

Keelan smiled. "Come on, let's eat." He told Teal. Then they made their way down an aisle of parked cars to the entrance of the Savoy.

"What's up, Keelan?" Chuck Sanders asked with his hand extended to greet the couple. "Who's this beautiful young lady?" Chuck Sanders asked.

"This is Teal," I answered.

"Nice to meet you, Teal," Chuck Sanders said.

"Nice to meet you as well," Teal replied.

"Welcome to Savoy. I got a good table for you two. It's close to the stage. We're having open mic tonight," Chuck Sanders said as he walked them through the low-lit Jazz club and restaurant.

"Okay, that's cool. Thanks," I said to Chuck Sanders.

"Here you go," Chuck Sanders personally sat the couple. It was something he only did for close friends.

"Good look, Chuck. If you ever need anything let me know," I told Chuck Sanders

"Just make sure your readers know about the place," Chuck Sanders said shaking my hand.

"Hol' up, is that Michael B. Jordan?!" Teal asked.

"Yea, that's him, Y'all wanna meet him?" Chuck Sanders asked the couple.

"YES!" Teal answered.

"Hmph, yeah, Chuck. That would be cool," Keelan said reading the excitement in Teal's eyes.

After taking a couple of selfies with Michael B. Jordan, Keelan and Teal took their seats.

A few seconds later, a waiter approached. "How are you this evening?" A tall white, blond, blue-eyed, and thin waiter with a wide grin on his face asked. Placing two Perriers, two glasses of ice, and two menus in front of them he asked, "Do you know what you're having?"

"Order for me, please, Keelan," Teal said.

"Okay, for the appetizer, bring us the Savoy Meat Balls and two Caesar salads."

"Alright, the veal/pork/beef blend and house made marinara, that comes with an excellent round of garlic bread, and two Caesars," the waiter said jotting down the order.

"For the main course bring us two orders of Wagyu-and-gras cheese steak, the butter-poached Lobster, and Caviar-spiked deviled eggs."

"And for drinks?" The waiter looked at me and asked.

"Bring us a bottle of Beringer."

"Cabernet Sauvignon. Alright, I'll be right back with the salads and appetizers. Should I bring the Cabernet now, or with the meal?" The waiter asked.

"Now."

Teal studied me as I took charge and ordered. She was feeling everything about him. "Thank you, Keelan," she said

"You 're welcome. Was that cool?"

"Yes, it was," Teal said.

So far Teal was everything I was looking for.

We sat and conversed about life. She told me that her two sons had different fathers. One was dead, killed during a drug deal gone bad, and the other one was somewhere doing time. It was the norm for little black boys to grow up fatherless where we came from, so we didn't dwell on the lack of black men in the hood. My divorce never came up, so I was cool.

God Send Me A Good Woman

After we had eaten while listening to poetry and song during open mic, we headed back to my place. We both had enough for the night and just wanted to enjoy more of each other's company. We canceled our plans of going to a club. Instead, we laid in each other's arms, watching *Pretty Woman* until I fell asleep.

Chapter 11

IT'S MORNING

It was seven something in the morning. I could feel my body shaking, and my name being called. "Keelan...Keelan ...KEELAN!" It was Teal. She had woken up, showered, and was ready to go pick up her kids.

"I'm up...I'm up," I said trying to focus.

"I gotta go pick up my kids. My sista called twice." She told me.

"A'ight, give me ah second," I said gazing at the angelic-like being whose face was overshadowed by the sprouting of the eye-searing sunrays glowing behind her like a halo.

It had been awhile since I had woken up to a woman's voice. Gathering my thoughts, I sighed, and rubbed my eyes. Finally, I realized that the date I had gone on the night before was real and not a fantasy. For some reason, it felt as though our night on the town was

145

imaginary. But it was the next morning, and I was being woken up by the beauty of my dreams. My yearning for love led me to believe I had experienced an outer body experience. Our date was too heavenly to be real. I thought to myself, yawning. Then I heard the Word of God speak to me:

'You were cleansed from your sins when you obeyed the truth, so now you must show sincere love to each other. Love each other deeply with all your heart. For you have been born again, but not to a life that will quickly end. Your new life will last forever because it comes from the eternal, living Word of God.'

"Did you hear that!" I asked Teal as she laid on top of me with her head on my chest.

"No! What?" Teal looked up at me and asked.

"Nothing," I told her, but what I heard was far from nothing. What I heard was God's Word clearly. It was 1 Peter chapter one, verses 21-23.

Before our date, I was acting like an ordinary man, and not as a spiritual man. I was living like a man of the flesh and because of this, I could not be fed solid, spiritual food. The pastor had fed me milk because I wasn't ready for the solid substance of God, the truth. Why? Well, because I was ignorant of life in the spirit.

Yes, I was contending for Christ, but yet I was flesh filled with jealousy, hate, and lust. I was dead through the trespassing of sin in which I walked by following the desires of body and mind. After my meeting with the pastor, my old, dead spirit was quickened into life, and my darkened and fallen spirit was made alive through being strengthened by the Holy Spirit. 1 Corinthians 3 explains how Christians are divided into two separate classifications the spiritual and the carnal, ones controlled by their sinful nature. Those that are jealous of one another and quarrel with each other. Yes, I was a born-again Christian, but I was still living like the people of this world. Instead of overcoming the flesh, I had been overcome by the flesh.

Now, I was feeling the Spirit dwelling inside of me. I felt as if it was controlling my entire being. I had received the spirit knowledge that allowed me to receive the spiritual life that dwelled inside of me.

The Pastor had used his holy sword and divided my non-corporal elements into dual parts leaving nothing to be hidden. The Spirit had become the ruling power in my spiritual resurrection. My physical body had been raised up with Jesus and seated with him in the heavenly places. Scholars have said that heaven dwells within the happiness of the mind, and in my mind heaven was in the company of a good woman.

The living and active Word of God used the two-edged sword to pierce through me and divided my soul and spirit from joints and marrow, discerning thoughts and intentions of the heart. I had been divided into dual parts. My date was a dualistic experience. It was as if God had sent his heavenly beings down, lifted me up and took me away like they did Ezekiel, or had carried me away by a whirlwind into heaven like he did with Elijah. It was as if the soul and spiritual, invisible parts of me had taken control of the visible outer corporal part of my body. Because I had become the master of my lust and sinful nature, I had become one with Christ, reconciled properly by means of his death on the cross. My hostility and sexual immoralities were put to death.

***

An hour had passed, I had dropped Teal off at her sister's, where we had parted with a kiss. Now I was back up praying after reading Our Daily Bread. What I read had confirmed what God had put on my heart. 1 Thessalonians 5:23-24:

'May the God who gives us peace make you holy in every way and keep your whole being spirit, soul, and body free from every fault at the coming of our Lord Jesus Christ.'

After saying my prayer, I stacked my Daily Bread on top of my Bible on my lamp stand and opened my Mac. I logged in to my Facebook page. I checked my notifications until I came to Teal Saunders, and clicked on her name. Looking over her page I saw that she had posted the picture we had taken with Michael B. Jordan. It had got 238 likes and 24 comments. I clicked on comments.

TEAL'S FACEBOOK COMMENTS:

-Oh, this is why I couldn't reach you this weekend.

-You, Keelan, Rockmon and Michael B. Jordan

-Teal, call me, girrrl!

After reading a few comments, I went to her photos. She had mentioned her baby daddies on our date, so I searched for them, and found one of her, her son and one of her baby daddies who was wearing a federal khaki suit on a visit. Then I searched for her other baby daddy and found him. It was a dated picture, I could tell by the quality of the picture, and the clothes he was wearing. I knew it was her baby daddy because the letters RWG was at the bottom of the picture. Then I studied another picture of Teal and her sons. I wondered how long it would take for me to meet them, the new *Star Wars* movie was coming out, and I thought about taking them to see it. "That would be the perfect time for me to meet them," I thought to myself.

I liked the picture Teal and I took with the young black movie star. I went back to my profile page and accepted the tag Teal had sent me of the picture we took. Normally, I wouldn't have because I knew how hateful people could be. How exes or haters like to sabotage the union between new couples that seemed happy. But I wanted this relationship and decided to let everyone know I wanted it, subliminally. Suddenly, I wished I could have erased all of my past relationships, and start fresh with Teal.

I clicked out of my Facebook page, went to my folders, and opened a file I titled: *Matters of the Heart.* It was my diary, but I struggled with the fact that I kept one, so I didn't address my personal journal with "Dear Diary," instead I used Matters of the Heart.

MATTER'S OF THE HEART (Log #378): My plans for a happily ever after may be close at hand. Recently I met with my Pastor, and he helped me gain a better understanding of what I was going through. Using the Bible, he pointed out the scriptures that enabled me to gain a new found spirituality. He basically taught me that in order for me to have a good woman and keep her, I would have to be a good man and use the Word of God as our bond. And my righteous deeds would sound proof this method.

"TEAL! TEAL! TEAL! TEAL!" I finally went on a proper date with a female name Teal, and our chemistry is amazing, she's amazing! She's God-fearing, owns her own business, a single mom with two little boys, and easy to talk to. She has completely piqued my interest. I've finally found someone healthy for me. My self-exploration may be over. I've let go of my anger, and I am back in pursuit of true love, and the hopes of building a strong, blissful relationship.

Our date night spilled into the morning, and our morning led to plans for another date. Besides that, we are going to church together next Sunday.

I can honestly say that I enjoyed our non-sexual date better than our sexual one. Not saying that her sex wasn't good because it was, I'm just glad that she had more to offer. With Teal, I expect to have a mature, meaningful relationship. A relationship built on something other than sex. A relationship that will last.

For months I have secluded myself. I built a wall of protection around my heart and withheld the key from my female companions. And they have done whatever they felt it would take to get to my heart. But up until now, I was not ready. Within the last several months I have had sex with a dozen, and couldn't find happiness. But now after one date with Teal, I no longer want to be uncuffed.

I'm emotionally prepared to invest in a relationship at this point. I'm ready to commit, to be locked down. In fact, if our next date is as good as our last, I will be willing to cut every other woman off. That's how strong I believe our compatibility is.

"What up with you?" I closed my Mac and answered my cell phone.

"Can you please tell, huh..." Wyoni had to look at the name tag on the doorman's work shirt. "Vincent, to let me up, please?" Wyoni said calling from the lobby.

"Hello, Mr. Rockmon." Vincent took Wyoni's cell phone and addressed me.

"Yea, you can let her up, Vincent," I told the doorman sitting my Mac on the lampstand with my Daily Bread and NLT Bible. I thought about Teal and then went to unlock my door for Wyoni.

"And where da hell have you been, and why haven't you been answerin' my calls, mister?!" Wyoni asked barging into my loft in a *Topshop* cable-knit scarf, checked cape, *Prada* ankle boots, and a *Dolce & Gabbana* shoulder bag.

"I was on ah special date, Wy. I had to shut the phone off," I told her.

"Ah date?! Ah date wit' who? Do I know her?" Wyoni was full of questions. "And when are you gon' give me the number to ya other phone?"

"That phone is for the job and my mother only. Ya not gettin' that number, Wy'. I'm definitely not givin' ya ass an all-access pass to bug me," I said.

"Yea okay! I'ma get that number one way or another," she laughed.

"Nah, ya definitely not," I said with a chuckle.

"So tell me about this new chic. Who is she?" Wyoni asked.

"Her name is Teal," I confessed.

"Teal from Click Ya Heels?"

"Yea. You know her?"

"She goes to our church, don't she?"

"Yea, and yea," I told Wy'. Our church held over two thousand members, and the Pastor did three separate services, so it was hard to know who all attended our church.

"Oh, she's pretty, Kee. I think we're friends on the Facebook," Wyoni told me. "Okay Kee, you got you, ah fly, church-goin' business woman," she said going into my refrigerator. "Why don't ya ass never have nothing to eat, Kee?!"

"Cause I always eat out. I'm never here," I told her.

"That's no excuse, Come on, I'm takin' ya ass food shoppin'."

"Fo' what? I'm good!"

"Come on!" Wyoni said grabbing her truck keys off of the counter,

***

At Giant's Supermarket on the Southside, Wyoni pushed a shopping cart down an aisle as I trailed behind her like a kid following his mother. As she started throwing things into the cart, I scrolled through my text messages and read a message sent from my ex-wife.

TEXT MESSAGE:

Payton to Keelan: Miss you. Please, call me, I would love to hear your voice.

"So tell me about ya date," Wyoni said examining food on the shelf.

"It was great. We went to ah baking class, and then we went to Savoy," I told Wyoni putting my phone away.

"Ah baking class, that was different. How was that?"

"It was fun as hell. I didn't think I would like it, but I did. You and ya young boy should come wit' us next time. We goin' again next Friday."

"Yea right! I'm try'na get rid of his young crazy ass. I'm mad as hell I took that boy to my house. I can't get rid of his ass. It's a shame that I can't even give out ah lil pussy without settin' off the psycho in ah nigga," Wyoni said with a little chuckle.

"Hmph!" I grunted, shaking my head. "Yea, these young boys are crazy out here."

"Yea, he just keeps poppin' up unannounced. I had to cut his ass off. No mo' pussy fo' him," Wyoni said.

"You crazy as hell, Wy'," I laughed.

"No! Fo' real. He keeps it up, he gon' meet my lil friend. That good ol' .380."

"Mmmmhmm, you out here driven 'em crazy," I teased.

"Yea, okay! He keeps it up his ass ain't gon' need no straight jacket, his ass gon' need ah body bag. Matter of fact, I know where he lives, I'm thinkin' bout putting ah separation order in on his ass."

155

"Fo' real? Doe Graham know about him?" I asked.

"Not yet. But if he keeps it up I'ma have to let the ol' guard dog, Graham, back into the house,

"Keelan?!" I heard someone call out my name. To my surprise it was Teal. She was shopping with her two little boys.

"Hey Teal," I said feeling awkward. She had just left my loft, and we were meeting again, unexpectedly, and I was with another woman. Wyoni and I were just friends, but she didn't know that.

"Hi, I'm Teal," Teal said to Wyoni."

"Hey, I'm Wyoni, Kee's friend."

"So this is ya little guys, huh?" I said trying to avoid the friend topic. Having a beautiful, well-built woman as a best friend was hard to explain,

"Yea.

"Hi guys," I spoke to the kids.

"Hi," said her two sons, Derek, and Brice.

"Your friend, huh," Teal said with a coy smile on her face.

"No, not like that, we grew up together. We're really just friends."

"I had to bring his ass shoppin'. He never has anything to eat in his 'frig," Wyoni said.

"Sure don't. I wanted to cook him breakfast, but there was nothing to cook. That nice ass house with nothing to eat in it," Teal said. I just listened to the two women talk about me like I wasn't there.

"I eat out a lot," I said trying to defend myself.

"Hmph, that's no excuse," Teal said.

"I told him the same thing," Wyoni chimed in.

"Hm, let me get the rest of my food. I'm thinking about having a guest over for dinner," Teal said looking at me with an inviting smile on her face. "Nice to meet you..." she said to Wyoni. "Call me," she said to me.

"Nice to meet you," Wyoni said.

"I really like her, Wy'," I said watching Teal and her sons stroll down the aisle.

"She seems cool," Wyoni said.

"She is," I replied hoping Teal didn't think that me and Wy' was messing around. Something like that could create unnecessary jealousy that could change things between us.

Chapter 12

CHOIR SINGER & THE FUNNY MAN

"Cuz, I'll see you at the shop." My cousin Larry told me in the parking lot of Bethlehem Church.

"Hope to see you at more of the services, cousin. Glad ya outta jail. Now all we gotta do is work on keeping you out." My brother told him. Then something or someone caught their attention. I turned to see what they were looking at, and it was Clarissa. She was leaning on my rental, waiting for me. I had avoided her since seeing her last, but this was one place I could not avoid her, church.

"I'll see you at the shop, bruh. Look like you might be ah minute." My brother had told me before he walked to his car, leaving me to deal with the beautiful choir singer with the mean look on her face.

I walked up to Clarissa with a grin on my face. "Hi Clarissa, wassup wit' you?" I asked hugging her.

"The question is, what's up with you, Keelan, or better yet, wassup with you and Teal? I saw y'all two buddy-buddy on ya page," Clarissa said with her eyes bugged out of her head.

"We went out on ah date and that's all," I said with a shrug of my shoulders.

"Yea right, Keelan. I doubt if that was all. I bet you had sex, did you have sex with her Keelan?!"

Clarissa's question caught me off guard. I had hesitated before I answered. In my mind, I was trying to figure out if I wanted this to be the end of her and I. I knew telling the truth could put a stop to what we had going on, and a lie would cause an argument but extend what we shared. I decided to tell her a half truth.

"DID YOU?!" Clarissa asked me again before I could answer. Looking sexy mad, her arms were crossed, sexy eyes were furrowed, and her luscious lips were twisted. In a crazy way, her rise of jealousy and suspicion turned me on.

"Yes, we had sex," I said.

"So that's why you haven't been answering my calls or messages? I've been replaced, huh?!"

"I wouldn't say replaced. We share something different than what Teal and I share."

159

"WOW! Are you serious? So what is that different thing that we share?" Clarissa asked starting to raise her voice.

"Calm down," I said looking around. "I'm not trying to hurt you. I'm just trying to be truthful. I respect you, so I have to tell you the truth."

"Oh, you respect me?!"

"Of course!"

"If you respected me, you would have spoken to me about you and Teal instead of avoiding me, before you shared that picture. Taking selfies with her an' shit!"

"Maybe that is something I would have done if we were a couple, but we're not Clarissa." I could tell that she was searching her mind for a legitimate reply to my response because she got quiet and just looked at me emotionless.

"I've been there for you, Keelan. I was there when you were going through your divorce and everything. I was the one you were talking to when you were down and out. She wasn't! I listened, I consoled you, loved you, and this is the thanks I get?!" Clarissa made some good points. She was the one that was there for me. I was always able to go to her.

"How could you do me like this after all the things we've been through together?"

"You right, you have been there, and I thank you for that Clarissa. But we've never established what we were doing, or what either of us wanted out of our relationship besides sex. You never told me that you wanted me to be ya man. All those times we've had sex you just let me walk out afterwards. You didn't say hol' up, Keelan! What are we doin' here?! I want more than just sex, you never did. So you can't get mad if I decide to have a relationship with someone else," I told her.

"Ew, shit! I feel used!" She said.

"Why?! I don't feel used. You got exactly what I got. If that's the case, then we've used each other."

"I'm saying I wasted all this time thinking that one day we would be a couple."

"But you never said that was what you wanted," I told her ready to let the whole situation go.

"But you knew that was what I wanted, Keelan," Clarissa said wrapping her arms around me, hugging me close. "I want you to be my man, Keelan," she said puckering her lips up for a kiss.

I kissed her. "'Rissa, I'm in ah relationship now," I told her, lying. Teal and I never established that we were in a relationship. I just assumed that was both of our goals, to eventually become a couple. The way I felt about a woman I only had sex with once and only dated once was insane. Here I was claiming Teal as my woman when she had not yet claimed me as her man.

Clarissa looked up at me. Her eyes turned a bloody red. "Ah relationship, after one date?!" She asked letting go and pushing me away. "FUCK YOU, KEELAN! YOU USED ME!"

"'Rissa?!" I called her name, and reached for her, but she backed away from me. For a second I looked around and noticed that people were watching as they exited the church.

"Nah, this is messed up. I waited all this time for nothin'. I could have been found me ah man," she cried.

"Come on, 'Rissa. Why you try'na act like I'm the only man in ya life?" I said.

"What you mean? You're the only man in my life that matters, Keelan."

"Am I?! What about the choir leader?! I heard about y'all."

"He's not my man. He don't mean nothin' to me. He's not you. I don't want him to be my man. I want you to be my man, Keelan," Clarissa said still trying to hold on to me even after I exposed one of her secrets.

"Clarissa, I'm not saying this to hurt you. I'm saying this to be as real to as I can be, I'm not try'na be in no rela…"

SMACK! Clarissa smacked the shit out of me before I could finish the word relationship.

"What the…Damn!" My eyes watered, and I tasted blood in my mouth. I held my face and saw stars. By the time the stinging stopped, and I had regained my focus, Clarissa was pulling off and giving me the middle finger.

***

Everyone at Oscar's Barbershop was laughing at me when I told them about Clarissa slapping me. I didn't tell them she slapped me because of my new girl, Teal. I just told them that I told Clarissa that I didn't want to be in a relationship with her.

"Boy, you got some bad luck with women," Cabby said.

"Yea cuz, you in bad shape in the woman department. There you go, cousin." My cousin said removing his smock from around my brother's neck and letting him out of his barber chair.

163

"Cuz, you act like your woman department is straight outta *Saks Fifth*. Just last month you were sleeping on my couch," I said climbing into his barber chair.

Everyone laughed.

"That is true, Lar'. Ya ass is always gettin' kicked out," Shane said laughing.

Everyone laughed including me.

CLICK! URRRR… My cousin, Larry, turned on his clippers. "Keep laughin' an' I'll run these damn clippers right up the center of ya head. Give that ass ah reverse Mohawk," Larry said aiming his clippers at my head.

"Come on, cuz!" I said laughing, and dodging his clippers at the same time. "See, I wasn't gon' do this, but now I gotta bring out my big gun.

"What you talkin' 'bout?" My brother asked.

"Yea, what the hell you talkin' 'bout, Kee?!" Cabby asked.

"I found my new wifey," I told the small group of men.

"Ya new wifey, though, cuz?" Larry asked spinning me around in his barber chair.

"Pull her up…Pull her Facebook page up," Shane said walking up to me chanting like a crazed rapper.

I pulled my phone out and navigated with my thumb to Teal's page. "Yoooo! Cuz, she baaaad!" Larry said.

"Yea, that's wifey material, bro," my brother said.

"Let me see, let me see," Cabby said reaching for my phone and taking it. "Oh, hell yea! She's tough."

"I seen her before," Shane said.

"She's ah member of the church," I told him.

"Yea, that's where I seen her," Cabby said.

***

"Sis, I seen ya new boo at church," Teal's sister Lizzie told her as she prepared Sunday dinner. They were at Teal's house on the Southside.

Teal smiled. "You did," she asked. "I told him that I was going out with him next week."

"His ass was hugged up, kissin' the choir singer in the church parking lot," Lizzie added.

"WHAT?!" Teal stopped chopping up veggies.

"Yea sis. I thought y'all had something special goin' on?" Lizzie said.

"I did too. I guess we don't. Especially if he's hugged up, kissin' another woman."

"Right! I was gon' say somethin', but I didn't feel it was my place to," Lizzie said.

"Sis, I'm glad you didn't. I don't need that type of drama. My days for that type of stuff is over. I'm not try'na fight, argue, none of that cause ain't no man worth that," Teal said moving her knife around in her hand as she spoke.

"I know, right? People out here gettin' killed bout that type of stuff nowadays," Lizzie said.

"DAMN! I thought he was the one. My someone special. And ah day after he hugging and kissing someone else. Matter of fact, that's prolly the girl I seen him with at Giant's when I went shopping yesterday." Teal was trying to put things together. "Is her name Wyoni?" Teal asked.

"I don't know, sis. I just know she be singing with the choir. Is she brown skin?" Lizzie asked.

"I don't know, whatever," Teal replied.

"But you said he was at Giant's with someone?" Lizzie asked.

"Yeah, talkin' bout it was his friend," Teal said.

"Friend my ass, sis. He was hittin' that!" Lizzie told her sister.

"Fo' real, girl! That's the vibe I got. They was acting too close. It was like they was married or somethin'," Teal said.

"So what you gon' do, sis?" Lizzie asked Teal.

"I mean, what can I do. He ain't my man. All I can do is ask him about it. Now if he lies, I'ma havtah cut his ass off , cause I don't play that lying stuff. I rather you cheat on me than lie to me. If you cheat and tell me the truth about it, I have the option to deal with you or not. But if you lie I can't respect you as a man. cause ah man stands up fo' his stuff, nah mean. Where my phone at? Let me call him," Teal told her sister.

***

"Hey Teal, wassup, baby?" I answered my cell phone, talking over the music playing.

"Where you at?" Teal asked.

"At my cousin Larry's barbershop, chill'in, gettin' my beard shaped up."

"BOY MOVE!" Cabby blocked Wyoni from entering the barbershop.

"Nah Wy', Sunday is just fo' men," Cabby told her.

"MOOOV-AH! Kee! Tell him to let me innnn!" Wyoni whined. "Soundin' like ah *Just For Men's* commercial," she said moving passed Cabby.

"Who's that?" Teal asked.

"Wy', my friend you met at Giants. My man ain't try'na let her in the shop," I told Teal.

"Come on, so I can finish. I can't shape you up while you on the phone, cuz," Larry said.

"A'ight. Hey Teal, let me hit you back," I said to Teal.

"Yea okay. Call me back cause I wanna ask you something," Teal said.

"Soon as I get out the chair," I told her.

"That's up bro. Welcome home! We missed ya crazy ass," Wyoni said to my brother.

"Hey sis, what's the latest?" My brother asked.

"Nothin', the same stuff that's been goin' on is still goin' on. You know what Proverbs say, *'Ain't nothing new under the sun'*," Wyoni said.

"How's my nephew? Tell him to call me. I gotta couple dollars fo' him," my brother said.

"He just came home on break. Shit! I'm glad you got some money fo' his ass. I'm goin' broke messin' wit' his butt," Wyoni said.

"Sis, don't worry, that football scholarship's gon' pay off big," my brother told Wyoni.

"Yea, and maybe he can buy me ah hundred and thirty thousand dollar car like that Audi RS7 you got sittin' outside. I know it's yours," Wyoni said.

"Come on, sis. You know how I do," my brother said to Wyoni.

"Boy, you just got out, mm mm mm. You some'in' else," Wyoni said.

"I got this Wy'. I'm good," my brother chuckled.

"Be safe, bro," Wyoni said shaking her head and giving my brother a hug.

"Hey y'all, my mom's having ah Christmas dinner fo' me around six o'clock on Christmas, I need y'all to stop over," my brother told everybody, and everyone agreed to show up,

"I'll be there, but I don't know what your nephew is gon' be doin'," Wyoni told my brother.

"I'll holla at him," my brother said.

"Hey, Kee?! Ya man's ah internet phenom," Shane said.

"Who?!" I asked.

"Cabby. You ain't watch that link I sent you earlier this week?" Shane asked me.

"Nah, I been meaning to. I'ma check it out now. What's it ah link of?" I asked.

"When Cabby was talkin' bout Adam and Eve. We uploaded it, and *YouTube* went crazy. I sent it to *GMA*. I'm waitin' fo' them to get back to me," Shane told me.

"*Good Morning America*?" I asked.

"Yea Kee. His word, not mine, got eight million views, and we got a little over ah million subscribers," Shane said.

"I see. This is big," I said.

"Let me see," Wyoni said. We all gathered around my phone and watched the video clip. We all started laughing, "This is funny as hell! "Wyoni said.

"We can develop this into ah TV show or somethin'," I said.

"You think so, Kee?" Cabby asked me.

"How much would that cost?" My brother asked.

"About ah hunid thousand," I replied.

"That ain't nothin', I think I can come up wit' that," my brother said. We all ignored his comment. He was the only one there that could consider a hundred thousand dollars as nothing. To us, that was like a million dollars.

"How big you think this could get, cousin?" Larry asked.

"Real big, Lar'."

"The views have dropped, though," Shane told me.

"Yea, because you only Vlogged once. Has anybody started promoting the page?" I asked.

"Naw. That's what we need you fo, Kee. You know how to do all that stuff," Shane said.

170

"I'll post it on my blog, and all my social media pages. I got over a million subscriber's too," Wyoni said.

"Thanks, Wy'," Cabby said. "No problem, bro," Wyoni said.

"We need ah set or somethin'. Do it like ah after dark talk show, you know, cuz?" Larry said.

"Naw, we can do it right here. Make it seem natural, real. Like the first one. You start glossing too much, too early, and you lose ya audience," I said.

"I feel you," Larry said.

"I know ah guy that works with *Maker Studio*. I did an article on him several months ago. I'll send the link to him, and see what he says," I offered.

"Shit sounds good, bro. I'm try'na invest my money in this here," my brother said.

"You talkin' bout shit soundin' good, it's soundin' better and better," Cabby said.

"Yea, it do Gab', but you need to post another video like the first one. Show possible investors that what you did was not ah fluke," I told Cabby.

"Oh bruh, I got material. It comes naturally to me. You know like that thing you goin' through wit' the two women? I got the Sarah and Hagar Story."

"Hol' up, Cabby. Let me get my phone ready," Shane said pressing record on his cell phone.

"A'ight, we good."

"Okay, here we go!" For close to forty minutes, Cabby broke down the story of Sarah and Hagar, homosexuality, and polygamy. It was great. Even better than the story he did about Adam and Eve. We asked questions and laughed while Cabby put on one of the funniest comedy skits about the Good Book I've ever heard.

After seeing Cabby perform, my brother took me to his house, and gave me two hundred and fifty thousand dollars; a hundred thousand for Cabby's show, a hundred thousand dollars to put up and fifty thousand dollars for myself.

"Fuck that paper job. This ya new job. Make this show work, and if you need any more money let me know." My brother told me.

My life was turning around, taking a change for the better. My brother was home, I found a good woman, I was hired to develop a TV show pilot, and I had learned to forgive all in a week's time.

Chapter 13

ONE TIME

"I can't believe you did this! Why Elaine, why?! Listen, I'll tell you what if your girl don't pay fo' my truck she goin' to jail, and maybe you too!" I said to Elaine standing inside of her house yelling at the top of my lungs, glowering at her. My verbal assault had brought her to tears, but I didn't care. I had never put my hands on a female. This was the closest I had come to doing so.

Earlier that Monday morning, the police had called me concerning the vandalism done to my truck. They asked me if I knew a female named Leslie Barnes. I told them that I didn't, but I remembered Elaine mentioning a friend named Leslie, so I went to her house to confront her and ask her if she knew a Leslie Barnes. Her response was, "Why?!" So I knew that she knew her, and was behind my truck being vandalized.

God Send Me A Good Woman

Frustrated, I said some things I would later apologize for, but I meant at the moment I was saying them. The more she tried to justify her actions, the angrier I got and lashed out with harsh words that ripped and shredded her to pieces,

At that moment, I wasn't hearing her cries for love or her need for a good man. There was a shortage of such men in our city, and she believed that she had found one, but I wasn't willing to be hers. Sadly, the more I made myself available, the more emotionally attached she became. The sex made things worse. For some reason, she assumed that her sex was an exchange for a long term relationship. But me, I wasn't looking at our hook ups as any kind of commitment, and that created a problem between us. My noncompliance to her availability made her take vindictive actions.

Me, on the other hand, believed that my problem was the damage done to my truck, but it truly wasn't. The problem was all the damage I was doing to the hearts of the women I was sharing myself with sexually. While I was yelling about a vehicle, Elaine was screaming about the emotional wreckage I had caused her heart to go through.

My sex was highly pleasurable, but also more destructible than a nuclear weapon. And no matter how dumbfounded to these facts I was, the women in my life believed that I knew exactly what I was doing when I was hurting them.

After exchanging profanities with Elaine, I stormed out of her house. As I sat in my rental, I tried to rationalize everything that had happened. Then my cell phone rang, it was Bella. "Yea," I answered.

"KEELAN, YOU BETTER COME GET'CHA BROTHER, FO' HIS ASS BE BACK IN THE PEN!" She yelled into the phone. In the background I could hear things being broken, my brother screaming some nasty things about his daughter's mother, and my niece crying.

"Put him on the phone," I told Bella, but my brother wouldn't get on the phone. "I'm on my way over. DON'T CALL THE POLICE!" I told her.

When I got to Bella's house, the police were there. The neighbors had heard the ruckus and called in the disturbance. Bella told the police it was all a big misunderstanding. I told the police that I would talk to my brother once I located him. They advised me that he stay away from the house for the rest of the day.

"Because if we come back here today, somebody in that house is going to jail," one of the officers said. Then he asked my name.

175

Normally, I would refuse to show my ID when I wasn't being accused of committing a crime, but I didn't want to cause another disturbance in front of my niece, so I gave the officer my name and ID. Then they went crazy. "GET ON THE GROUND!" They demanded. "You're wanted for assault!" One officer said.

"THE ASSAULT OF WHO?!" I asked trying my best to stay composed believing that it was all just a big misunderstanding.

"YOU'RE ARRESTING THE WRONG MAN!" Bella wailed.

"Elaine Edwards! We heard the call put out over the radio on our way over here," the arresting officer said putting his handcuffs on me and pulling me up from the ground.

"YOU'RE ARRESTING THE WRONG MAN!" Bella wailed again.

"MA'AM, BACK UP, BEFORE YOU GO TOO!" The other officer said to Bella.

"UNCLE KEE! UNCLE KEE!" My niece cried out. Seeing her crying out in tears upset me and brought tears to my eyes.

"I DIDN'T ASSUALT HER! What are you talking about?!" I said.

176

"SAVE IT FOR THE JUDGE!" The arresting officer said shoving me into the back of the police cruiser.

***

It took almost eight hours for me to see the judge. I was released on my own recognizance. It was the first time in my life that I had ever been handcuffed, tossed into the back of a police car, and locked in a holding cell with a dope fiend that smelled like shit, a drunk that vomited all over himself, a murderer, and a crazy man that talked to himself while pacing back and forth.

I thought about my brother and my crying niece the entire eight hours of my incarceration. I thought about the drama my niece had gone through and all of the time my brother had done. I had a new found respect for him. Being locked up was something I never wanted to experience again, and he had experienced it twice. It really made me want to make Cabby's show work so that my brother could leave the streets alone.

"What the hell, bro?! My fault. I ain't mean to get you locked up," my brother said to me after I got into his car.

"It's not ya fault, bro," I said. "Damn, when you get this," I asked about the new Audi RS7 my brother picked me up in.

"The other day. You like this shit?" He said. "Hell yea! This is tight," I told my brother.

"Damn! My fault, bro," my brother apologized again.

"I told you it wasn't ya fault, bro," I repeated.

"What happened then? Whose fault was it? Bella feels bad as shit. She feels like it was all our fault and I do too," my brother said.

"Nah, some broad named Elaine got me locked up. She told the police I beat her up," I told my brother taking my cell phone out of my plastic property bag.

"Bro, you don't hit women."

"You know I don't. She just mad that I stepped to her about bustin' the windows on my truck."

"Oh, she did that? You talkin' bout that one chick, whose house I picked you up from?"

"Yup, she had her girl do that to my truck." When I turned on my phone, my email, and message alerts sounded off back to back. My mother, job, Wyoni, Teal, and dozens of others had tried to reach me. I rubbed my forehead thinking of Teal. I was supposed to have called her right back on Sunday, but I had gone home and fell asleep. Now this. I didn't know what she would think about my arrest for assaulting a woman. No one likes a woman beater. Even though I was innocent, that was my charge, and that's all that people would consider, my charge, not my innocence.

My brother watched me shift in my seat, sigh, and began to stress. "I can't believe this shit!" I said, frustrated. I wanted to call Elaine, but I didn't want her to go to the police again. I was stuck, and I didn't know what to do.

"I can take care of this fo' you, bro." My brother said as I scrolled through my messages.

"Nah bruh, I need you to stay outta trouble fo ma's sake," I said dialing my mother's number. "Hi, ma...Yes, I'm okay. I'm with Dorio now...A misunderstanding...Yea, that's all...No! I'm not going to prison...Yes! I will be cleared of all charges...Okay, love you," I said hanging up.

"Yea, you will be cleared of the charge one way or the other, straight up!" My brother said. I looked over at him and shook my head. He knew I was looking at him, but he didn't look back at me because he knew I didn't want him getting into any more trouble, but he wasn't trying to hear that. My freedom and everything else was on the line with my arrest. He had a hundred thousand dollars invested in a show that he believed only I could develop, but not only that, he wasn't ever going to allow anyone to take my freedom.

Thinking about it all, I figured the only way to dead the situation was to go at it from the source. Scrolling down my messages, I stopped when I came to some unopened messages from Elaine, and one included a picture. I opened it. It was a picture of Elaine, battered and bruised. Her neck was scratched as well as her face. Her text message read:

Elaine to Keelan: Don't ever threaten to put me in jail.

As I read Elaine's message, Wyoni called, "Yea Wy?" I answered.

"You okay?" Wyoni asked.

"Yea, I'm good," I lied.

"Did you see the post about you on Facebook?" Wyoni asked me.

"Nah, I haven't been on there yet, what it say?" I asked her.

"Some chick posted a picture of herself with scratches and bruises all over her face and neck. She saying you did it."

"What da fu...No, she didn't, Wy'?!"

"Her post says, 'This is what you get when you try to break up with Keelan Rockmon.'

"Man this broad is crazy!" I said.

180

"What bro?!" My brother asked. I showed him the Facebook post.

"Yooo! This bitch is crazy, but I got somethin' fo' her crazy ass!" My brother said.

"Wy', let me hit you back, that's my job calling on the other line."

"Call me back, Kee, seriously. And do not go messing with that chick! Stay away from her crazy ass," Wy' said to me.

"Wy', I ain't do this shit!"

"Kee! I know you didn't, you're not into that. I know you!" She said.

My job had hung up before I could answer. I would deal with them later. I had to call Elaine. I needed to find out what was going through her head.

I attempted to call Elaine several times before she answered. "WHAT KEELAN?!" She screamed into the phone.

"Elaine, why are you doing this to me?!" I asked.

"I'm not doin nothin', you are, you're doin this to yourself. All on Facebook takin' pictures wit' bitches," she said cold and callous.

I ignored her comment. I knew she was talking about the picture I took with Michael B. Jordan and Teal. "Why you tell them people I beat you up. What you do to yourself?" I asked Elaine.

"You did this to me!" She replied.

"Come on now, Elaine! You know I ain't put me hands on you! You playing games with my life," I told her.

"Keelan, you the one that said you was gon' put me and my friend in jail," Elaine said.

"Elaine, you know damn well I wouldn't do nothing like that, but you did it to me. Got me booked on some bogus ass charges, and you posted some bullshit all on Facebook, got me looking like ah woman abuser an' shit!"

"That's what you get for pressin' charges on us," Elaine said.

"I DIDN'T PRESS NO CHARGES ON Y'ALL! I told the police I didn't know her!" I yelled. The line got quiet, and I could her Elaine crying and sniffling.

"Bye, Keelan!" Elaine said, hanging up on me.

I tried to call her back at least ten times, but she refused to answer, so I decided to let her cool off. I would wait for her to call me back, and I knew she would eventually.

Then my ex-wife, Payton, called. I pressed end. I didn't feel like explaining what happened to her.

"What she say, bruh." My brother asked when he saw that I had stopped trying to call Elaine back.

Then Wyoni called, and I pressed end.

"She mad about ah picture I took with Teal," I told him.

"What bruh?! Fo' real?! All this is about ah picture?" My brother asked me.

"I guess. For real, though, she mad I ain't try'na be wit' her ass."

"Another one of them? Didn't you just get smacked about not wanting to be with ah chick, bruh? What the hell you be doin' to these joints?"

My brother asked with a smile on his face, but I wasn't in the mood to laugh. Then Teal called. "Hello?!" I answered on the first ring.

"Hey Keelan," she said and paused. "What's all that stuff on Facebook about you beating someone up for leaving you?" Teal asked.

"That's all ah lie. I didn't put my hands on her, and we weren't together," I said looking at my job's number flashing on my cell phone's LCD screen. "Damn! Teal, that's my job. Can I call you back?"

"Whatever. Nah, you know what Keelan, don't call me back." Teal said frustrated by what she had heard, seen, and me always having to call her back.

"Hello?" I answered the call from my job.

"What is all this stuff I'm hearing about you abusing a woman because she broke up with you, Keelan?" Mr. Crawford, my ex-wife's father asked me.

"Mr. Crawford, this is all ah big misunderstanding. Some girl beat herself up, and told the police I did it, but I didn't. I never touched that girl. We argued, but I didn't put my hands on her," I told Mr. Crawford.

"Big misunderstanding or not, I got'ta let you go, for now, Keelan."

"Are you serious, Mr. Crawford?!"

"I can't have anything like this tied to the paper. I would be subject to all kinds of scrutiny. So until this matter is cleared up, I have to let you go," Mr. Crawford said.

"What about freelance jobs?" I asked.

"Bro, hang up on that ma'fucka! You ain't gotta beg fo' shit!" My brother said, but I ignored him. I really wasn't trying to lose my job. I had worked hard to get where I was at, and I wasn't trying to lose everything because of a lie.

"Sorry, no association at all. I have to get rid of you until this gets cleared up. Sorry, Keelan."

"But you know I'm not like that! I don't abuse women. All that time Payton and I was together I never raised my voice at her. And you know all the crazy stuff she put me through," I pleaded my case.

My brother got angry, hearing me beg for my job, but it was all I had going. I couldn't go make two hundred and fifty thousand dollars on the streets like him, so I didn't care about his attitude. All I cared about was my job.

"Keelan, my decision stands. I'll tell you what when this gets cleared up, I'll give you your job and position back. Now I got'ta go, sorry," Mr. Crawford said before hanging up.

Pulling into the garage of my building, me and my brother sat in silence for a few minutes.

"So he fired you, huh?" My brother broke the silence.

"Hell yea. Mr. Crawford said that the paper can't be associated with a woman abuser."

"But he knows you're not ah woman beater. I can't stand his ass! All the things you do for that paper. If it wasn't for you that black-owned newspaper wouldn't exist anymore, it would have been out'ta business," my brother said.

185

What he was saying was true. If it wasn't for me implementing fresh ideas, and a social media presence, Mr. Crawford's company would have been out of business.

"Well bro, you know what you got'ta do. You gotta focus on our show. You got'ta make them regret that they let you go."

"No bro! I need to focus more on God, worry about nothing, and pray about everything. That's what the Bible says," I told my brother.

"Bro if that's what you feel like you got'ta do, and that makes you happy, do that. But trust me, I'm not gon' let you go to jail," my brother said, but what he didn't realize was it wasn't up to him, it was up to God.

Chapter 14

JOB 1:8

Doing close to 100MPH, an ambulance with the sirens blaring, transported Wyoni's body to Allegheny General Hospital. Inside, medics placed an oxygen pump over Wyoni's mouth and nose and manually pumped oxygen into her body trying to force it into her bloodstream and brain. Pushing fast, deep and hard, they broke two of her ribs doing one hundred chest compressions per minute in an attempt to restore her heart rhythm. At the same time, they were trying to prevent the ventricles from pumping blood into the lungs. Knowing that ventricular fibrillation could cause a cardiac arrest, they used good medical judgment, and continued cardiopulmonary resuscitation, working feverishly to revive her.

Wyoni's body began to shake and flutter. It failed to sustain a regular heartbeat. As one medic resumed CPR, the other used a needle-tipped drill to penetrate the shinbone. Next, he inserted an IV line into the vein-rich tibia to produce a direct route for sedatives and other medications. Waiting and watching tentatively, the medics waited for Wyoni's tightly clenched jaw to relax. Then they fitted a combitube down her esophagus into her airway. Once the tubes were inserted, the EMTs turned on a rich supply of oxygen and administered epinephrine followed by amiodarone to combat any irregular heartbeats. Finally, using the V-Fib three times, and Wyoni's heart jumped back to rhythmic life. After giving Wyoni another dose of amiodarone into the combitube, they used the V-Fib once more. The EMTs were pessimistic. One second, two seconds, three seconds later, the heart monitor beeped once, twice and then continually. Wyoni's heart surged back to life by beating on its own.

Moments earlier, Wyoni was removing Christmas gifts from her Mercedes-Benz GLS and taking them into her Mount Washington home. "Avery, come help me get these gifts out of the truck," she yelled up her steps to her son. He was in his room, playing Black Ops online with his schoolmate, Brucie.

"A'ight, hol' up, ma. Here I come!" Avery hollered back.

188

"BOY! PAUSE THAT DAMN GAME, AND COME HELP ME, OR YA ASS WON'T GET

NOTHIN' FO' CHRISTMAS ...AAAH! Jamal, what are you doin' here?!" Wyoni asked her young sex partner.

"So you gotta a PFA out on me, huh, bitch?!" Jamal asked close up in Wyoni's face.

"Look Jamal, you cannot keep poppin' up on me like this. My son is here."

"I don't give ah fuck who here. If ya ass would start actin' right, I wouldn't have to pop up, or worry bout ya son seeing me cause I would be livin' here. But it's too late now..."

"Jamal, please don't do this," Wyoni said seeing Jamal pull a 9mm from his hoodie.

"Cause you try'na play me an' shit. You think cause ah nigga young you can play me!"

"Jamal, baby, don't!" Wyoni said dropping her gifts from her hands, turning, and running. She tried to escape the crazed street thug, but she couldn't.

"POP!" Jamal shot towards the back of Wyoni's head. The shot made her collapse to the ground. Her blood immediately began to leak from the back of her head.

"MAAAA!" Coming down the steps, Avery and his friend, Brucie, saw- his mother being shot in the head as she tried to run away from the gun-toting maniac.

As Avery ran to aid his mother, he used his phone to call 9-1-1.

His friend, Brucie, ran to the door to see if he could get a description of the shooter. When he looked outside, Jamal was taking Christmas gifts from Wyoni's SUV, and putting them in his vehicle. Seeing Brucie watching him, Jamal got in his car, and abruptly pulled off.

"D-Q-Z 5-2-1-7," Brucie said trying to memorize Jamal's license plate number.

"What?!" Avery asked him.

"Red Hyundia Sonata, his license plate number is D-Q-Z 5- 2-1-7."

***

A group of us waited for permission to go see Wyoni. Besides my mother, she was the strongest woman I knew. Our mothers sat together. I sat with the barbershop crew, and my brother sat talking to Avery. We both loved Avery as a nephew. When we first arrived at the hospital, Avery was visibly upset, nervously shuffling around. I watched him as I massaged my hands together. I didn't know what to say to him. My brother took him to the side and calmed him down.

Seeing the Director of Trauma emerge from a back room, we all stood. "How is she, doc?" I asked.

"Are you her husband?" The doctor asked, making everyone look at me.

"Nah, just family," I replied.

"I need to talk with somebody that's in the patient's immediate family," the doctor said looking around at the small crowd of loved ones.

"I'm the mother, just say what the hell is goin' on wit my Wyoni. I ain't got no time to play no games with you, boy!" Wyoni's mother said.

"Alright," the doctor said studying Wyoni's medical records on a clipboard. "The operation went well. God was definitely with her cause she should have been dead."

"The devil's a lie!" My mother said.

"She's recovering now. She may not be responsive for a few days. Of course, we had to give her a lot of medication, so she's heavily sedated. She will have to go through a few more operations, but for the most part, she's a survivor. She survived what us doctors call nonsurvivable."

"Well, my God is powerful. He is a deliverer, ah miracle worker," Wyoni's mother stated.

"AMEN! HALLELUJAH! THANK YOU, JESUS! PRAISE YA HOLY NAME!" My mother felt the Spirit moving in the hospital. Her eyes were closed, she shook her head, and stomped her feet.

"Yes, your God is a powerful God cause like I said, she shouldn't be here right now."

"When can we go in to see her, doc?" I asked.

"Ah, you can go in now, but please go in two at a time. Just for now. And tomorrow, like I said, we'll be taking her in for surgery again," the doctor said.

"Doc, let me ask you a question. What do she gotta go back to surgery fo'?" I asked.

"Well, we removed the bullet from her, but there are a few fragments that we saw on the X-rays and CT Scans, and we want to remove as much of that as we can. And also we want to repair some of the damage the projectile did to her skull," the doctor told us.

"Oh, okay, doc. Thank you," I said.

"Alright, please have a good evening folks."

***

After a long night at the hospital, I went home to take a shower. While there I took out my Bible, and began to

192

praise God. My body trembled, and tears came to my eyes. I no longer had control over myself. The Spirit had overcome me, and I spoke in tongues. I thanked my God, the Almighty, and all powerful, Yeshua, for saving my best friend.

KNOCK! KNOCK! KNOCK! KNOCK!

Someone was knocking at my door. Inside, I wished it was Wyoni coming to bug me, but I had just left her. Thinking of her, I could see her laying in the hospital bed, full of tubes and IVs.

KNOCK! KNOCK!

"YEAH?"

"Hi baby. You miss mommy?" Mereza asked standing in my doorway.

I slammed the door in her face.

KNOCK! KNOCK! KNOCK!

"Keee-lannn, open the door!" I heard her saying.

Using the phone, I called down to the lobby. "Vincent…"

"Keelan! KEELAN!" Mereza called out.

"Why you let this woman up here?" I asked the doorman.

"KEELAN!"

KNOCK! KNOCK! KNOCK! KNOCK!

193

"I always let her up, Mr. Rockman," the doorman reminded me.

"Well…for future reference, her all access pass has been revoked. Now send security, please." I told the doorman.

"Right away, Mr. Rockman. Right away!"

Chapter 15

JOB 2:10

"Should we accept only good things from the hand of God and never anything bad?" Job 2:10

KNOCK! KNOCK! KNOCK!

I had just fallen asleep when I heard someone knocking at my door.

KNOCK! KNOCK! KNOCK!

"Damn! This better not be Mereza again!" I said throwing my Goose Down comforter to the side of me. Shirtless, in my silk pajama pants, I walked to the door.

KNOCK! KNOCK!

"WHAT?!" I yelled, then I stood back shocked.

"Hi, Keelan David Rockman. I see you been taking good care of yourself," she said gently clawing her manicured hand across my bare chest. "Can I come in?" She asked politely.

"Yeah Payton, of course! This is your house, too."
Yes, it was her, my ex-wife.

"I would have called, but I knew you wouldn't have answered. So I just came as soon as I could. How is she?" Payton said asking about Wyoni.

"Her speech is slurred, and her vision is blurred in one of her eyes, but she's alive."

"THANK GOD! I had just got off the phone with her. I was talking to her when she pulled up at her house, and then this," Payton said with a deep sigh, exhaling air from her mouth.

Both in deep thought, neither of us spoke. It had been months since we had been around each other.

"Have you been getting my messages?" She asked after a few minutes of silence leaning against a wall with her arms crossed.

"Payton, to be honest with you, I haven't been getting your messages because when I see a message alert from you or a call from you, I don't answer. So no, I don't be getting your messages," I said trying to stand my ground and trying to hurt her at the same time.

"What about the messages I give to Wy to give you?" She asked.

"She tries to give me ya messages, but I told her to quit bein' ya messenger. And she still tries to be, but when I hear your name, I cut her off before she can finish."

"Why? You acting like I'ma murderer," Payton said taking a few steps from the wall towards me.

"You are. A murderer of hearts," I told her taking a few steps backwards as if to warn her not to come closer.

"Oh, I am? Really, Keelan?!" Payton said moving passed me to sit on the *Elan* sectional. I took a seat across from her.

"So I've killed the love in you, murdered the sensitive side of you, eradicated your line of communication, shot dead the forgiveness in your heart, and stuck a knife in your kindness. Keelan, you go to church, and you read the Bible, and pray every day. Can I ask you a question?" She said.

"Yes, of course."

"What does the Bible say about forgiveness?" She asked, and I knew that I was treading on thin ice.

"It says a lot about forgiveness." Deep inside I hoped that she would keep the Bible out of our conversation. She knew God's Word better than me. She was the one that convinced me to accept Jesus Christ into my heart, and to become a Christian.

"Specifically, let's talk about Matthew 6:14-15. It says, *If you forgive those who sin against you, your heavenly Father will forgive you. But if you refuse to forgive others, your Father will not forgive your sins.'* When Jesus taught the disciples to pray, he taught them to recite these words, *'And forgive us our sins, as we forgive those that sin against us,'* in verse 12, and Jesus says in Mark 11:25, *When you are praying, first forgive anyone you are holding a grudge against, so that your Father in Heaven will forgive your sins, too.'* And what about 1 John 4:20-21 where it says, if someone says, *I love God, but hates a Christian brother or sister, that person is a liar; for if we don't love people we can see, how can God, whom we cannot see?* And he has given us this command, *Those who love God must also love their Christian brother and sisters'.*"

Payton had used God's Word against me. How could I discredit her without denying the Word of God? I couldn't. "And what does it say about homosexuality?!" I hit her low, below the belt. It was my only defense at that point, but Payton was too smart to turn a discussion about God's Word into an argument. The truth was, I was still angry about catching her in bed with another woman.

"The same thing it says about those who indulge in sexual sin, idol worshippers, adulterers, greedy people, thieves, drunks, prostitutes, abusers and cheats, none of us

198

will inherit the Kingdom of God. But be careful, Keelan, because Galatians 6:1-3 says, *'If another believer is overcome by some sin, you who are godly should gently and humbly help that person back onto the right path. but be careful not to fall into the same temptation, yourself.'* It tells us, *'To share each other's burdens, and in this way obey the law of Christ. Because if we think that we are too important to help someone, we are fooling ourselves. We are not that important,'* you want me to continue husband?"

"Go 'head," I said bracing myself for the tongue-lashing she was putting on me using God's Word.

"Romans 2:1 teaches us that we may think that we can condemn such people, but we are just as bad, and we have no excuses! When we say they are wicked and should be punished, we are condemning ourselves for we who judge others do these very same things. See husband, you still condemn me for things God has forgiven me for. I've been calling and calling; sending message after message, trying to ask for your forgiveness. Keelan, we don't have to be married to love each other. My sinful nature has harvested decay and death. It killed my marriage, our friendship, our trust, and our love. It's the murderer, not me, Keelan, but since our divorce, I have been living to please the Spirit so I can harvest everlasting life. When it comes to us, it seems like we got tired of doing what was good. Not just me, both of us, and that's why our marriage stopped harvesting blessings. Galatians 6:10 teaches us that whenever we have the opportunity, we should do good to everyone. Especially to those in the family of faith. So husband..." Payton moved close to me. "Would you please forgive me?" She asked.

I sat there thinking for a couple of seconds. "Yes Payton, I forgive you. And I'm sorry for not giving you the opportunity to apologize sooner," I said, with my head down.

"It's okay. I'm just glad we've finally had a chance to talk. Look…" Payton went into her $17,000 *Bermes Rouge Pivone Togo Birkin*, and pulled out a letter. "I wrote you a letter. You don't have to read it now. Whenever you feel the time is right to read it, read it. Now…" She started saying, handing me the letter, "can I have a hug?" She asked.

"Okay," I said, hugging her. "Mmmm, I miss my husband," Payton said.

***

Everyone was gathered at the hospital excited to see Payton and myself come to the hospital together. In

Wyoni's hospital room, we held hands with our family and friends around Wyoni's bed, and Payton lead us in prayer.

"Oh God, whom we praise, don't stand silent and aloof while the wicked fight against us for reasons known and unknown. They repay evil for good and hatred for our love. Fill our hearts with confidence so we can sing your praises with all of our hearts. Lord, help! When we call on you as we cry in trouble, and save us from distress, calm our storms to a whisper, and still the roaring waters, change our deserts into rivers, and make our salty wastelands, fruitful, fortify our faith, so that we bring glory to your name and Kingdom, Father, in our distress we don't call on man, for no human can help us, so we call on you, Lord, because only your help can do the mighty things we pray for, so we call on you, Father, to heal our sister, Wyoni. We call on you, Father, to remove our wicked ways, and we call on you, Father, to protect us from those that are violent, those that plot evil in their hearts, in Jesus name I pray, Amen."

After Payton prayed for us, I took her to the airport where the BNN company jet awaited her. On the way there, I got her caught up on everything current in my life, Teal, the assault charge, the new show, and her father firing me. She made me promise that I would read her letter when I felt the time was right.

Chapter 16

JESUS, SAVE US SINNERS

"Can we stay home tonight/try something new tonight/this drink got me feeling right/I'm bout to lose my mind," DeJ Loaf rapped.

DeJ Loaf featuring Lil Wayne, *Me U & Hennessy* played as Teal drove us to my loft in her white-on-white CT6. I laid back, reclined in the passenger seat listening to the lyrics, and thought about how right Teal was for me. I was feeling eh'thang about her. Payton always told me if I ever dated anyone to make sure she was on her level or better, and Teal was definitely up there. A beautiful entrepreneur with her own money.

We had spent the afternoon shopping for Christmas presents, at her expense. "What else you want?" Teal asked, pulling clothing off of the racks she wanted to see me in, and that was after she bought me a *Louie* trench coat, belt and shoes at *Ross Park Mall.*

After we shopped, we ate at the Cheese Factory where we talked about my ex-wife, Wyoni, and Clarissa and the truck incident. I was completely honest with her. She called for a new start but warned me.

"No more drama, or else," she said, with a meaningful smile on her beautiful face.

"'No mo' drama, promise," I replied.

"Can we stay home tonight/ try somethin' new tonight/ don't wear ya thong tonight…" Lil Wayne rapped.

***

We arrived at my loft, and I dropped my shopping bags down on my bedroom floor. It was around 8:30 pm, on a Saturday. Teal and I planned on getting cozy, spending Saturday evening watching a movie, and talking.

"Where is it?" Teal asked.

"What?!" I asked feeling confused.

"The tree, bae!"

"Oooh, it's in the closet out there," I said. Before I could explain exactly where my Christmas Tree was, Teal bolted off in search of it. I had told her that I had bought a tree, but because I didn't have kids or anyone to spend Christmas with I never took it, the lights or ornaments out of their boxes.

Wanting to get comfortable, I stripped down to my wife beater and put on a pair loose fitting pajama pants.

"Come on!" Teal said coming into my bedroom as I looked through a Best Buy bag for the movies we brought home to watch.

"Ew, I wanna get comfy," she said, coming out of her *Valentino* pumps and *Eric M.* bodysuit. "Hand me that." She wanted my V-neck t-shirt. "You want some Henny?" She asked slipping my t-shirt over her lace *Balconette* bra and panties. She looked so sexy. I watched her full of lust as she pulled the bottle of Cognac out of a *State Store* bag.

"Naw, I'm good. I don't really mess wit' that," I told her.

"You not gon' have a shot wit' me? Come on. Quit being a killjoy, babe. I'm helping you put ya tree up, and you ain't gon' have a shot wit' me?" She said flopping down on the bed, resting up against me.

"A'ight, I'll have ah couple shots wit' you."

"Let's make this fun," she kissed me and said.

"Anything for you, babe."

"Anna-ee-thang?"

"Yea."

"Come on, let's put the tree up," she said, reaching for my hand.

With a smile on my face, I let her drag me into my living room to have shots and put up my Christmas tree.

Two hours and several shots later, the Christmas tree was put up and decorated with a black angel on top of it. Teal and I laid in my bed, watching *Think Like A Man.* Kevin Hart was hilarious.

Teal's head rested on my chest. The Henny had us feeling right. Between scenes, we held small talk about her store. I listened as she spoke, rubbing my chest. As she talked, I thought about the great sex we had before we started dating. "So what are we doin' here Teal? Are we dating, or are we just havin' fun?" Normally, females asked me this question. I felt strange asking it. It was the first, but you know what they say, 'It's a first time for eh'thang.'

"Are you asking to be my man, Keelan?" Teal asked me.

"I'm just sayin', I really like you," I told her.

"Well, I'm really not into dating men without a job..." She joked. When I told her about the truck situation, I also told her about me getting fired. "But I might make an exception for you, only if..." she paused and looked up at me.

"Only if what?" I asked.

"If you give me ah massage," she said lifting her head from my chest.

"Oh, consider it done," I said rising up.

"No! I'm not gon' consider it done. I wanna feel your hands all over my body," she said slipping my tee over her head.

"I got just the right thing for this," I said looking for the heating oil Mereza had left behind.

"What?!" She asked curious to know.

"Some oil that heats up as I rub it into the skin. Here it go," I said. Pouring some into my palm, I rubbed my hands together and started massaging Teal's back.

"Mmmm...Oh...Hmm. Keelan, ah...Ah, that feels soooo good," she moaned as she looked back at me biting her bottom lip. "Get my legs," she said.

I poured some oil on the back of her legs and started massaging it in. "You like that. It feel good?" I asked.

"Hell yea, baby. Go up..."

"Right here?" I asked, moving up her leg. "Up…"

"Here?"

"Up," she said opening her legs like a pair of scissors.

I took two hands and massaged her upper thigh. I could feel the warmth and wetness of her on my hand. Then I started massaging her ass cheeks.

"You like that fat ass?" She asked looking back with her eyes slanted.

"Mmhm," I hummed pecking each of her ass cheeks. Temptation was getting the best of me. I fought it with prayer last time, but this time ,I didn't want God to save me from sin. This time, I would just have to repent. Moving downward, my warm, wet kisses made her moan.

"Mmmm...Damn bae, that feels so good. Don't stop," she said.

Sliding my fingers through the two hills of her bottom, I drove them into the abyss of her moist darkness. Slipping them in an out of her set off a fire deep inside of her core. Her bodily fluids moved fast to put out the cause of the flames she felt between her legs, drenching my fingers with a wetness that had a cherry scent. My mouth drooled, my tongue wanted to taste her pinkness, and I wanted to make her cum in my mouth. But before I could, she stopped me.

"No, come here," she said guiding me to lay me on my back. Pulling the string on my pajama pants, she loosened them and pulled my pants and briefs off. My dick popped up like a Jack-in-the-box. "Oooh, I remember you," she said running her tongue up and down the sides of it. As she did this, she finger fucked herself enjoying every lick of my erected prick.

"Shiiit!" I hissed. Her soft, slimy tongue made me confess the pleasure I felt. Then she ran it down the base of my shaft to my balls, sending a tingling sensation throughout my body. "Mmmm," I moaned as I grabbed a handful of her jet black hair and balled it into my fist. I pulled her head back, making her open her mouth. "Put it in ya mouth, all of it," I told her.

"I can't," she lied.

"Put it in ya mouth!"

"Kay, I'll try, daddy."

"Good girl."

As she took me into her mouth, my body tensed up, and my ass cheeks clinched as she slid my dick smoothly between her thick lips down her throat.

"Cah...Cah...Slluup, slluuup," she gagged, slurped it, and made drool run down the sides of it."

"Aaaaaggghh! Agh...Ah," I growled.

Then she took her small hand and stroked it hard, slamming her mouth down on as much of it as she could. Looking me in the eyes, she circled her tongue around the crown of my dick. I moaned out shaking my head as my eyes rolled into the back of my head. Then she climbed on top of me and put my dick inside of her. Her pussy lips slid down it, dripping juices all over it. She rolled and popped her hips harder and harder. I grabbed her by the waist and guided her in a circular motion.

"Ah...Ah...Yes! Yes!" She said with clenched teeth.

"You like that dick...You like that dick?!" I asked as she rode me.

"Love it...Love...AAAGGHH, I'm cumin' on it...I'm cummin' on it," she said as her stride slowed down.

I started pounding her pussy, thrusting my hips with everything I had in me. "SHIT! SHIT! Ah yes, baby! Mmmm...Mmmm!"

"Oooh, you cumin' in me. You cummin'," Teal said collapsing on me.

Laying there, we both were exhausted. Our heavy breathing blended with the sounds of the TV. Wrapping my arms around her, I felt like I was in love.

***

The next morning, Teal had woken up before me and woke me up to breakfast in bed.

"What service we gain' to?" She asked.

"Damn, I was out, huh?"

"Yea, I did that," she said with a smile on her face.

"Shut up," I said with my eyes still closed.

"Come on, bae, eat. we gotta get ready. What service we gain' to?"

"The ten O'clock service," I said scooting up in bed to eat breakfast. "Good sex, good cooking, and a good woman. This what I need in my life," I thought to myself.

***

Flocks of parishioners in their big brims and Sunday best meandered into the Coventry-style cathedral at Bethlehem Church for ten o'clock service. While a light rain fell, melting what little snow that was left on the ground, they shuffled underneath umbrellas and suit jackets held over their heads to the church doors. Tracking their feet in high heels and dress shoes through puddles of unvarying downpour into the Lord's House.

Bethlehem Church was launched in 2013 from my Pastor's living room. He and his wife started with seven members, and that seven members grew into a powerful mass and volume of one million spiritual warriors and a 29,000 person congregation that tuned into his weekly podcast and Christian blog. They expanded one church into several tabernacles with lofty tower house offices, lecture rooms and other facilities, including gymnasiums for after school activities.

God Send Me A Good Woman

Pastor Pops Thomas was a beckon of light in the darkest depths of the black community. A convicted felon and ex-heroin addict that met God in a jail cell somewhere in Huntington, Pennsylvania, he married his wife during that three year stint, and together they converted 5000 inmates to Christianity.

Small groups of faithful members gathered, greeting and conversing amongst each other throughout the church. Eager to get to our seats, Teal and I, allowed the usher to escort us down the aisle to the pew I usually sat in with my family and friends. Happy to see my brother and Bella at service, I hugged Bella and smiled and nodded at my brother.

After the announcements, the choir stood in their Purple and gold choir robes as Clarissa made her way to the microphone to sing lead. Seeing her adjust her mic stand, the choir director readied himself by putting his hand and button in the air.

Clarissa started with a humming-riff, "Mmmmm...Hm...Mmm..."

The organ and piano players played slow and steady with their fingers as everyone awaited Clarissa's first note. Then her angelic voice rang out. "Ev-en-though your wings blow..." She started singing as the bassist strummed, and the drummer drummed a slow and steady beat. Some of us stood, clapped, and put our hands to the sky, praising Jesus as Clarissa sung, *'I Told The Storm'*.

"I-I want you to know-oh..." she continued.

"THANK YOU JESUS! THANK YOU JESUS!

"HALLELUJUAH!"

"YES!"

The congregation praised Jesus.

"GO 'HEAD, GIRL!!" Teal said.

"THANK YOU, FATHER!" I cried and raised my hands filled with the Holy Spirit.

"You caaa-ause me nooo-o a-larm, cause I'm safe in his arms..." Clarissa sung, uplifting the church.

"HALLELUJUAH! HALLELUJUAH!"

"MM MM MM!"

"GLORY TO HIS NAME!"

"HALLELUJUAH!"

The congregation praised Jesus' name.

By the time Clarissa started the third bar of the song, the entire congregation was standing, including the pastor's and their wives.

"Be-cah-ah-ah-ause of faith, I have a brand new day/the sun will shine-ine/and I-e-I-e-I will be okay/that's what I told the storm," Clarissa sung the lyrics choppy but heavenly melodic. Her voice gave me chills and my arms goosebumps.

"I-TOLD-THE-STORM TO PASS STORM YOU' WON'T LAST GO A-WAY I COMMAND YOU-TO-MOVE-TO-DAY," the choir sung the chorus, swaying their bodies back and forth. We shouted and praised, giving God the glory for fifteen minutes after Clarissa stopped singing which caused her to do an encore.

Then the choir was seated, and Pastor Thomas approached the podium with his iPad. After he gave his opening prayer, he instructed us to turn our Bibles to Matthew 21:18-22 it was the story about Jesus and The Fig Tree.

"May you never bear fruit again! And immediately the fig tree withered up," Pastor Thomas read the scripture and then, he started preaching

"When Jesus comes to you, don't you dare not produce! When Jesus comes to you hungry or thirsty, don't you dare not feed him or quench his thirst! Because Jesus curses and withers those that bear no fruit. What am I sayin'? I'm sayin' do not let Jesus closely examine you and your religion has no substance, or your faith is without works. Because faith without works is dead, like a body without breath," the pastor preached.

214

Fifty-five minutes later, Alter Call was called, and my brother walked up to the front of the church where a couple others stood to dedicate the lives to Christ.

"I'm proud of you, bro," I told my brother, hugging him after service was over.

"I'm really try'na change my ways, bruh," he told me as we stood in the parking lot of the church.

Then the craziest thing happened. As Teal and her sister talked with Bella, Clarissa walked up to Teal. "Hey gurrl, you did ya thing..." Teal said to Clarissa, thinking she was coming to say hi.

WHOP! WHOP! I ain't try'na hear that shit, you took my man!" Clarissa said, hitting Teal twice.

Before I could even react the fight was happening in the parking lot of the church. "Stop y'all, we at church! Stop! Stop...CLARISSA! What is you doin', grab them, bro!" I yelled out as soon as the shock wore off.

After Clarissa hit Teal, Teal and her sister started jumping her. Bella tried to break the fight up, and me and my brother helped separate them.

"I'M DONE! I'M DONE! YOU HEAR ME?! I'M DONE, KEELAN! SHE CAN HAVE YOU!!" Teal yelled as people gathered around, shaking their heads, and whispering about what had happened.

"This ain't no damn club!" I heard someone saying as they pulled off.

"I KNOW I CAN HAVE HIM, HE'S MINE!" Clarissa said as she broke away from my restraint.

"CLARISSA! GET YA BUTT OVER HERE, NOW!!" Clarissa's mother, Big Pam yelled out. "WHAT THE HELL ARE YOU DOIN', FIGHTING AT CHURCH?" She said to her daughter. Clarissa looked at me with her nose flaring and her eyebrows bunched together.

"Why you do that? That was crazy!" I said, picking Teal's *Giovannio Harlyn* Big Brim up from the ground.

"Like I told her, you're mine!" Clarissa said.

"Girl! GET YA ASS AWAY FROM THAT WOMAN BEATER," Big Pam said, snatching her daughter by the arm.

"I'm not ah woman beater, Ms. Pam!" I said in my defense.

"Whatever, Keelan! Stay away from my daughter," Ms. Pam said.

"Oh, no problem. You just tell her to stay her crazy ass away from me, straight up!"

"Damn bro, the pastor, is looking over here at you," my brother told me.

I looked up, and the pastor was walking towards me.

"Brother Keelan?"

"Yea?" I said putting my head down. I felt ashamed. I had cause a fight at the church.

"You okay?" The pastor asked.

"I'm tryin' pastor," I said looking up at him.

"Well, if you need to talk, call me. We can get together again," he told me, never saying a word about the fight.

"Pastor, I just want a good woman. I think I had one, but I just let her go," I said.

"God will send you one. You just gotta recognize her when he does. Now call me when you get ah chance," the pastor said shaking my hand and pulling me in to embrace me.

"Okay Pastor Pops," my brother said shaking the pastor's hand.

"Alright, make sure you brother calls me. I'll be praying for you boys," the pastor said walking off to hold a conversation with some other believers.

***

When I arrived home, I looked over at Teal's Hatinator and dialed her number.

"HELLO?!" She answered.

"TEAL?" I said sensing hostility in her tone.

"Keelan, I meant what I said. I'm done with you. I ain't got time for that nonsense, fightin' at the church. I'm so embarrassed!"

"I know, I'm sorry?"

"Don't be, Keelan. Just don't ever call me again..."

"What about ya..."

CLICK!

"Stuff." Teal had hung up on me mid-sentence. My past cost me a good relationship, and I knew she was serious about never wanting to hear from me again because she didn't even ask about her things.

My brother asked me what I was doing to the women in my life. My question was, "What are they doin' to me?!"

Chapter 17

THIS CHRISTMAS

On Christmas, my mother did what she could to keep smiles on me and my brother's faces. The *Temptation's Christmas* usually played while my mother baked and cooked the holiday meal.

During this time of year, on the cold days of December, the Steel City was normally covered in snow, and it's Three Rivers were frozen. But that never stopped the holiday shoppers from shuffling in and out of stores, searching for deals, gifts, wrapping paper and bows in downtown Pittsburgh.

As vehicles slowly drove passed slow and steady, flinging snow and salt at the feet of cheerful pedestrians, Macy's played Christmas carols that filled giving hearts with the holiday spirit.

This Christmas was a very special one to my mother because both of her sons would be having Christmas dinner with her. My brother's incarceration, normally, stripped the happiness out of what most people considered to be the joyous holiday of the year.

That morning, family and friends gathered around Wyoni at the hospital, so that she wouldn't feel left out or saddened by not being able to attend the Christmas dinner. My mother and hers brought her aluminum foil-wrapped plates of food, and Tupperware bowls of dessert. We prayed and sung Christmas carols to lift her spirits. Everyone was just happy that she was still alive, and by the grace of God, she was having a speedy recovery. We all knew that her surviving the gunshot to the head was a miracle. I promised her that I would Facetime the dinner, and would be back to visit her in the morning.

Several hours later, everyone had started arriving at my mother's Christmas decorated house. Some people watched the game and drank beer while the kids drank eggnog and ran through the house playing, or secretly seeking out their names on the presents awaiting them underneath the large evergreen tree, illuminated by Christmas lights, and a glowing angel on top of it. My brother, Avery, and Avery's friend, Brucie, were in one of the rooms upstairs playing *Black Opts* online, and my cousin Larry and Shane played chess while Cabby watched.

Me, I sat on the steps talking to Wyoni. I was trying to keep my mind off of Teal not being there. I hated the fact that my past relationships had ruined my chances of a new one with her, but what could I do? Even worse though, I hated the thought of my best friend, Wyoni, being alone. Without a job, I stayed at her bedside, working on my new book or Cabby's after-dark talk show, *Barber Cheers*. It was a mix of the latest music, mixed drinks and barbershop gossip.

We bounced ideas off of each other and shared our black books and go-to people with one another. We had even paid for a set to be built so that we could have an audience. Cabby's second video, *The Sarah and Nagar story Remixed*, strengthened his following. The video had got five million views in one night, and in a week, he had gained an additional one million views. Scheduled to be on GMA, the Today Show, and the Steve Harvey Show, we readied ourselves to launch on our YouTube channel.

At times, Wyoni, struggled with depression. She had dedicated her life to creating opportunities for young black males like the twenty-six-year-old career criminal that had shot her, and that's what really bothered her. The bullet passed through her hair and skin, indented and entered her head, fractured her skull scattering the projectile's fragments through delicate tissue, and bursting rigid holes through blood vessels and brain cells that were healthy only moments before. It ripped a jagged vortex of destruction through the brains gelatinous lobe. The shooter's bullet then exited the side of her cranial bone. But by the grace of God, only days after being shot, Wyoni's brain resiliently withstood the brutal damage and began to mastermind its reconstruction.

The doctor said that the slur in her speech and the blur in her peripheral vision would improve with the help of physical therapy, but her nightmares and suffering would continue from the lasting memories of her being shot. Her attacker, Jamal Glenn, had been captured only minutes after the shooting, thanks to the fast thinking of Avery's friend, Brucie.

The day after Payton had come to town to see Wyoni, Teal also went to the hospital with me to see Wyoni. "You really love her don't you?" Teal asked me.

I nodded my head, "Yes," holding Wyoni's hand with chocolate tears running down my brown face.

Our mothers were close, but after this family tragedy, they became closer. Her siblings constantly cried when they visited, and Wyoni's ex-boyfriend, Graham, visited once and never returned.

Avery was staying with my brother until his mother got better, or until he had to return to school. The incident made him want to drop out, and stay home to help his mother. But On Deck convinced the second stream quarterback from Ohio State with the 3.8 GPA and 1350 SAT score, to stay in school to pursue his career. On Deck had even put ten thousand dollars up for him.

"Spend this shit wisely, and don't draw attention to yourself. Fuckin' up ya NFL chances. Don't be buying six hundred pairs of Jay's and designer clothes try'na impress ma'fuckas," my brother told Avery.

Hanging up with Wyoni, I headed into the kitchen and gave my mother's frail but beautiful face a kiss. She turned her cheek to receive the kiss. "Take this to the table," she told me, handing me the golden brown turkey on a silver platter. Then my brother came in the kitchen behind me, and stuck a fork into the baked macaroni and cheese mixed with chunks of lobster and shrimp, SMACK!

"Take it, an' sit it on the table, boy!" Wyoni's mother said, smacking my brother's hand.

As Donnie Hathaway's *This Christmas* played, everyone pitched in to set the table. We had turkey and mac and cheese, cranberry orange relish and fried mashed potato patties, sautéed bean casserole, lamb biryani,

223

molcejas en escabeche (chicken gizzard and banana salad), greens, sweet potato pudding, rigatoni with turkey meatballs, pork sausage and melted cabbage, oysters with cocktail sauce and lemon slices, and white wine to go with it, for those that like a little buzz with their meal, there were gobble-gobble tini's (cranberry juice, prosecco, and vodka, garnished with orange zest with a side of frozen cranberries to chill. For desert, we had Momma's special banana pudding, orange Jell-O mold, SHOO-Fly pie and cherry slab pie. All that food sat on the huge dining room table. We ate like kings and queens. I ate until I had to loosen up my belt, and unbutton the button on my jeans.

"Bro, we goin' to see that new *Star Wars* joint. You try'na go?" My brother asked me.

"Nah bruh. I'ma help Ma wit' the kitchen, and I'ma head over to the hospital and sit with Wy'. Plus, I need to tighten up ah few screws on the show," I told my brother.

"Bro, ya ass is working. How that set comin' a...Holl up, bro, let me answer this. Hello? Yea, where you at? I'm headed to the show. I'll stop over on my way...bet!" My brother put his cell phone in his pocket and picked up my niece. She walked up to him, and started pulling on his hand until he hung up the phone, "'Sup Dookie?!"

"Ew daddy, don't call me that!" My niece said as my brother picked her up. "Mommy said I can't go. I wanna go, daddy!"

"You wanna go?"

"Yea, I wanna go, daddy," my niece said giving my brother the sad eyes.

"Aight, you goin' then," my brother said giving in easily.

"Dor', no! Her butt is gon' be sleep!" Bella said trying to have a little bit of time with my brother for Christmas.

"Unc', we rollin' out. We headed to the club," Avery said to my brother. Then him and his friend shook my hand. "Love y'all," he told us putting on his coat to leave.

"Be careful out there, Av'. Keep ya eyes open. You know how them haters get," my brother told Avery.

"So yo, bro, I'm out. But tomorrow I wanna go see that joint," my brother said to me, talking about the set we had built for the show.

"Got you," I said to him standing up to give him a hug. "Love you, bro. Don't worry 'bout the show, me and Tidy' all on it," I said.

"Nah, I ain't worried about it. I know you got me, bruh. We bout to get this bread. I'ma leave the streets alone. I'ma move into a bigger spot, and collect paper..."

"We ready," Bella said, zipping my niece's coat up.

"A'ight. But yea bro, see you tomorrow," my brother said.

As I picked up my plate to take it into the kitchen, my brother called me.

"Keelan?!"

"Yea bro," I turned. and said.

"Love you, big bro! Eh'thing gon' be aight!"

I paused to look at my brother. He looked peaceful. The way he did when we were kids. "Love you too!" I told him back.

"Dorio, take these plates with y'all. Bella, come by tomorrow, and get whatever's left cause I'm not try'na have all this food go bad," my mother told my brother.

"A'ight we gotta go, ma. We try'na catch this movie," my brother said.

"Okay, go 'head. Love you," my mother said, giving them all a kisses while I just watched.

"Love you, grandma," my niece told my mother.

"Love you, too, baby," my mother replied.

"A'ight bro," I said one final time. My brother looked at me and smiled. It was good to finally have him home where he belonged, and I was going to make sure he stayed.

Rae Zellous

Chapter 18

JOB 1:12

"All right, you may test him," the Lord said to Satan. "Do whatever you want with everything he possesses, but don't harm him physically."

I'ma stop over Arab's fo' ah second. He got some money fo' me," On Deck told Bella, pulling onto Columbus Avenue.

"I hope you ain't got no drugs in the car with our daughter, Dorio," Bella said looking back at their daughter, Doraine, sleeping in the back seat.

"Come on now! You know I ain't wit' that shit. I'ma get this paper and let him know I'll bring the work in the mornin'. Look, you just focus on that big ass rock I put on ya finger. Matter of fact, I may as well get that back cause you acting like you don't know how this marriage thing gon' go. I'ma be runnin' shit. The man in the marriage tells the woman what to do," Dorio said opening up his car door.

"Yea right! Whatever, you got life messed up. This ain't the old days," Bella said shifting in her seat.

"Aight now, mess around, and that ass won't be gettin' married," On Deck said playfully.

"WHATEVA! Go boy! The movie about to start," Bella said rolling her eyes with a smile on her face.

"I'm in and out. Be right back promise," On Deck said getting out of his car and going to his friend Arab's door. "Open up da do'," On Deck said, talking to Arab on the phone.

A few seconds after On Deck was in the house Bella started seeing strange men step out of the shadows of dark parked cars. Then she noticed that the strangers had guns in their hands. Squatting down, they positioned themselves behind their car. Watching everything unfold, Bella, slowly pulled out her cell phone from her purse, and tried to call On Deck, but as her phone rung, the LCD screen on On Deck's cell phone lit up, blinking off and on. It was in the cup holder on silent. He had accidently left it in the car.

"Damn! Dorio," Bella said. Realizing that she could not call him, and warn him, she started videotaping what she was seeing.

***

"You sure you don't want this now?" Arab asked On Deck.

"Nah, I'ma head out North Hills to the movies. You know they be trippin' out there. I ain't try'na have all that paper on me," On Deck said.

"So you gon' bring that work tomorrow, though?" Arab asked.

"Work! What you mean work? You didn't say you wanted ah job wit' my brother's new company. You just said you was try'na invest in the show," On Deck said with his hush-finger up to his mouth, and a mean mug on his face. He was advising that Arab play along with him.

"Oh nah. Nah, I…Well just get the money in the mornin' that's straight," Arab said nervous and afraid. He knew that On Deck had a quick temper, and he kept a gat on him to back it up. What he didn't know was On Deck's semi-automatic weapon was in the stash box inside of his car.

On Deck looked harshly at Arab for a few unsettling seconds letting him know that he knew he was trying to set him up. He had noticed the same strangers parked outside that Bella noticed. But to him, they weren't strangers. He knew exactly who they were, DEA agents.

Preparing himself to be rushed and tackled, On Deck took a deep breath and stepped out of the front door with his hands fully visible.

"FREEZE!

"PUT1CHA HANDS UP!"

"POP! POP! POP! POP!" At the same time, special agents were yelling different demands another one of them was firing his weapon. Pumping his service slugs into On Deck, blowing his body back into the doorway of Arab's house.

"DOOOORRRR-EEEE-OOO! DO-REE-O! DORIO!" Bella's wailing woke up her daughter and made the special agents surround her car.

"PUT'CHA HANDS UP...LET ME SEE YA HANDS!" The special agents demanded, and Bella complied.

"Why you shoot him? Why-did-you-shoot-him? He wasn't doin' nothin'. I need to call his brother!" Bella was screaming as the special agents pulled her from the car and started searching it without her permission with her daughter still in the backseat. Little Doraine, looked at the special agents with a terrified look on her face.

"Let me get my daughter! LET ME GET MY DAUGHTER!" Bella said as the special agents searched her and her purse finding nothing incriminating.

After Bella got her daughter, she ran over to On Deck's lifeless body but was stopped several feet from him by other special agents. She heard another special agent calling for the Allegheny Medical Examiner.

"Hold up, ma'am. You can't go up there!" A special agent said holding his arm out.

With her arms wrapped tightly around her mother, Doraine, looked back at her father lying in the doorway. "Daddy? Daaad-dee? Get up, daddy. I wanna go to the moo-vees. Mommy, is daddy okay?" Doraine asked her mother, confused about everything that was going on.

***

I was putting on my coat. I had just finished helping my mother and Ms. Roselle, Wyoni's mother, clean up when my phone rang for the third time. Digging into my coat pocket, I pulled out my cell phone and answered it. Before I could say 'Hello,' I heard someone screaming into the receiver, "DORIO'S DEAD, KEELAN! YOU HEAR ME..."

Hearing those words froze me in my tracks while everything else was moving around me. My mother was talking to me with a smile on her face, and Ms. Roselie was laughing until my plate crashed to the floor.

"KEELAN, THE POLICE KILLED YOUR BROTHER!" Bella said.

CRASH! My plate hit the floor spilling food and dessert onto the wooden panels. "What do you mean my brother's dead?! Y'all just left!" I asked. My mother and Ms. Roselie paused, attentive to every word I said.

"Jesus, no! Please don't!" My mother pleaded as her legs wobbled. Ms. Roselie braced herself as feeling of sickness swept through her stomach. Each hoping what they were hearing wasn't true.

"Ma, the police killed Dorio..." I blurted out.

"Let me see that phone...Hello?!" She said after taking my cell phone.

"Ma, the police shot and killed Dorio coming out of his friend's house for no reason," Bella told my mother.

"Where are you?" My mother asked.

"1021 Columbus Avenue."

"We're on our way," was all I remember hearing my mother say. Till this day I don't know how we got to the crime scene.

***

Wyoni, was watching the Channel 13 News. Fishscale was also watching Channel 13 News while sitting in the dayroom of FCI Beckley.

"Breaking News: Man that has been identified as Dorio Rockmon..." The newscaster started saying.

"...Was shot and killed by officers conducting a controlled buy as he was coming out of a house on Columbus Avenue on the North Side of Pittsburgh..."

Wyoni's heart dropped. She picked up her phone and dialed my number.

"...Rockmon was on his way to see the latest *Star Wars* installment and decided to visit a friend to wish him a Merry Christmas on his way to the movies. But Special agents believed that he was there to sell the owner of the house drugs, and when he left out his friend's front door he was shot and killed by the special agent that believed he was reaching for a weapon..."

Hearing On Deck's name, Fishscale got out of his seat and moved closer to the TV. When he heard that his friend had been killed, he stumbled backwards and fell over his plastic prison chair.

***

"Yea Wy'?" I answered my cell phone.

"I'm watching the news...Don't tell me they killed my brother?!" Wyoni said.

There was a long silence between us, and all you could hear was the commotion in the background from the scene of the shooting, sirens, reporters, civilians and the police.

"Yes...Snst, snst, he's gone, Wy'. I'm lookin' at his body," I told my best friend. I was being as strong as a man could be in this situation, but truthfully, I was tore up inside.

"Naaawww...Mmmmm...Mmmm, snst, snst, Whyyy is this happening? Why is all of this happening to us?" Wyoni cried out.

"Let me call you back, Wy'."

CLICK! I had to hang up with her. I couldn't take hearing her suffer. Why was all of this happening was a question I was also asking myself.

As we stood there behind yellow tape, we waiting for the Allegheny County Medical Examiner's to load my brother's cold body into the

Coroner's van. A small crowd of twenty or thirty people began to grow into one or two hundred people. Bella had uploaded the video of my brother being shot with the address on her social media pages and supporters and non-violent non-profit groups started to arrive and gather around the scene.

Officers from around the city and nearby departments were called in to help maintain order.

Three hours later, I was at the AGH hospital with Wyoni. She held me as much as her wounded body would allow her to. Bella was there also, calling around and accepting calls, putting together a peaceful, spiritual walk to memorialize my brother's death and bring awareness to the police brutality that was going on in the city of Pittsburgh.

My mother, Ms. Roselie, and my niece went to my mother's house. As my niece slept, my mother and Ms. Roselie started making funeral arrangements.

My brother's smiling face was etched in my mind. His last words, 'Love you, big bro! Eh'thang gon' be aight!' Echoed in my head. I felt lost and helpless without him, but I refused to let my brother die in vain.

Chapter 19

NO JUSTICE-JUST US!

BNN INTERVIEW WITH PAYTON CRAWFORD-ROCKMON:

"Olivia Rockmon, a resident of Pittsburgh's Southside, experienced unimaginable grief after a video went viral of the murder of her son. On this video her thirty-eight-year-old son, Dorio Rockmon, was shot and killed during an alleged drug deal as he walked out of a friend's home on Christmas night. Now the mother and her eldest son, Keelan Rockmon, are on a mission to ensure their community will not endure another incident like this again. And today Ms. Olivia Rockmon and Keelan Rockmon are joining us via satellite to talk about her son, the shooting, and their new movement, R.A.I.S.E U.P., Rights Against Injustice Seeking Equality Uplifting People. Thank you for joining us."

"Hello Payton," Ms. Rockmon greeted.

"Hi, thanks for having us," I spoke.

"Thank you. Um, I have a report here that says that DEA agents were assigned to investigate suspected cocaine distribution activity between the victim and an unknown suspect. Initially, they were focused on the unknown suspect that claimed Dorio Rockmon was his supplier. During surveillance of the unknown suspect's apartment, they observed Rockmon pull up and enter the apartment. And upon leaving he was shot and killed because it was believed that he reached for a weapon. Basically, they're saying that this was just a drug deal gone bad."

"This was no drug deal gone bad. This wasn't even a drug deal, but it was definitely wrong. My brother was not at his friend's house to sell drugs. He was there to wish his friend a Merry Christmas," I answered.

"So where does the information about the drug deal come from?"

"There was an informant giving them false information in order to gain leniency," I answered.

"So does your brother sell drugs?"

"He was a convicted felon and has served time for possession with intent to deliver. But since his release a couple weeks ago he seemed to be on the right path. He was working, going to church, and he had recently dedicated his life to Christ. But regardless of all of that, in this case, there were no drugs found on him, in his car or in the house he was visiting." I replied.

"So..."

"Hold on, Payton, let me finish. There were no drugs. And let me add this when the DEA does these so called 'controlled buys,' they give the informant documented currency to exchange with the distributor that's being investigated. There was no recorded currency on my brother. So where do they get off saying my brother was there to sell drugs?" I was heated reliving my brother's tragic death and the lies they told.

"But say he was there to sell drugs, which he wasn't, but say that he was. Does that give the police the authority to murder my son? No, it just gives them the authority to arrest him, and if he doesn't comply with their demands, they have the authority to restrain my son, not kill my son," my mother stated.

"You're absolutely right, Ms. Rockmon."

"You know it sickens me that we live in a society that's so acceptable of lives being taken over senseless matters. The police killed my son for walking out of his friend's house. The officer says my son was going for a weapon. My son didn't have a weapon. Furthermore, there was nothing even remotely close to a weapon on my son. He didn't even have his cell phone on him."

"Speaking of his cell phone, the footage that went viral was taken by his girlfriend on his cell phone. We have the footage, and I would like our viewers to see this footage. If it's not too harsh for you," Payton thoughtfully asked.

"No Payton, show it. It hurts to watch it, but the world needs to see what the police is doing to our kids," my mother humbly replied.

"Okay viewers, I have to warn you that the footage that we are about to show is very graphic.

"FREEZE!"

"PUT'CHA HANDS UP!"

"POP! POP! POP!"

"DOOOORRR-EEEE-OOO! DO-REE-O! DORIO!"

"PUT'CHA HANDS UP...LET ME SEE YA HANDS!"

"Why you shoot him? Why-did-you-shoot-him? He wasn't doin' nothin'. I need to call his brother."

There was silence.

"From what I saw in the video, your son comes out of the house with his hands visible. I never saw him

240

reaching at all, and you say there were no drugs involved?" Payton questioned.

"No drugs were involved! They killed my brother. They killed him on Christmas in front of his fiancée and daughter," I reiterated.

"The hurt I feel inside from losing my beloved baby boy has been unbearable," my mom silently cried.

"I can't imagine what you're going through, Ms. Rockmon. Right now we're showing the uprising that happened yesterday not only in Pittsburgh but Nationwide. Allegheny County's Top Prosecutor, Tom Mckensie, cleared special agent, Jake Rowney, of any wrongdoing in the shooting death of Dorio on Christmas day. The Commonwealth Attorney, McKensie, said in a letter that his office 'finds no basis for further criminal investigation into the death of Mr. Rockmon'. And y'all took to the streets shortly after hearing that?"

"We had to for my brother's sake. I can't let him die in vain."

"Do you feel that violence and looting justify your brother's death?"

"Not at all. We don't want violence. We don't want any more people hurt. That's why I'm here. That's why I'm on your show to speak out against it. VIOLENCE TOOK MY BROTHER!'"

"Great! So today the R.A.I.S.E U.P. movement is having a peaceful, Stop Police Brutality rally in Pittsburgh. Can you tell us more about it?"

"Yes. Um, leaders of all Pittsburgh communities will gather all supporters from their neighborhoods, and begin to march to downtown Pittsburgh where we'll all meet up at City Hall around six o'clock to hear the voices of those that are demanding social change and uplifting. Basically, whoever wants to stand up at the podium and give a positive speech will be able to," I provided.

"From what I'm hearing you're calling it 'The Justice for All Speech'."

"Ah, that's something that my friend Wyoni came up with. I guess we can call it that. A day after my brother was shot and killed by a narcotics officer, I went to see Wyoni, and wept in her arms. Tragedy had struck twice and only left one survivor. God had spared her life. Miraculously she's recovering, getting her vision and speech back. But the death of our brother would ripple pain through a sea of us. His daughter will grow up as another fatherless daughter like Wyoni, but my brother's absence will have a different effect on her. Instead of being angry at a man because she never had a true one in her life, she will grow up afraid that a true one will love her and then leave her. This will only be one of the psychological affects her father's death would have on her. Her age will allow her to have some memories of her dad, but he won't be there when she will need him the most. He will just remain in her head as a tragic story of how she lost her dad on Christmas. Because of this, Christmas will never be the same. The holiday in itself will forever have a mix of good and bad emotions in her psyche. Her heart will yearn for him to be there when she learns how to drive, graduate, walk down the aisle, and have her first child. She will never go without. I'll make sure of that. Her and her mother will split my brother's share earnings of *Barber Cheers*. So she will never have to worry about finances, but that will not replace her father, not even I can do that." I closed out the show.

Later that day, I sat, balled up in the corner of my shower, full of rage and vengeance. The very two things I had let go of when I forgave Payton. I had been there for over an hour screaming and yelling curse words at the officer that took my brother as if he was there. His bullets had caused all of this. I could not believe that they were on the news calling him a good man. To me, he was the devil or worked for the devil. His actions showed the world that he killed my brother for no reason. "Is this another test, Father?!" I cried out to my God.

Finally, making it out of my self-pity, I gathered myself again as a believer. The Bible taught me that whatever happened it was God's will. *"God causes everything to work together for the good of those who love him and are called according to his purpose for them."* Romans 8:28 played in my head. Then as I laid still on my bed, Jesus spoke to me.

"Don't be afraid of those that threaten. For the time is coming when everything that is covered up will be revealed, and all that is secret will be made known to all. What I tell you now in the darkness, shout abroad when daybreak comes. What I whisper in your ear, shout from the housetops for all to hear! Don't be afraid of those who want to kill your body; they cannot touch your soul. Fear only God, who can destroy both soul and body in hell." And right then, I let go. I felt a great burden lifted from my shoulders.

Feeling my body starting to tremble, I fell to my knees, completely naked, and I thought about a scripture in the Book of Job, Chapter 1 verse 21, *"I came naked from my mother's womb, and I will be naked when I leave. The Lord gave me what I had, and the Lord has taken it away. Praise the name of the Lord!"*

In all of this, I did not sin by blaming God. "Echoe, play *Let Go*, by Dewayne Woods. I quietly listened as the song began to play.

> *I couldn't seem to fall asleep*
> *there was so much on my mind...*
> *So then I kneeled down and prayed…*
> *Then he said you don't have to cry*
> *cause I'll supply all your needs.*

"THANK YOU, JESUS! THANK YOU, FATHER!" I cried and praised.

> *As soon as I stopped worrying*
> *worrying how the story ends*
> *when I let go and I let God*
> *let God have his way*
> *that's when things start happening*
> *when I stopped looking at back then*
> *when I let go and I let God*
> *let God have his way...*

As I praised, my phone alerted. It was a message from Elaine. I hadn't talked to her since the day of my arrest.

Elaine to Keelan: I'm so so so sorry to hear about your brother. My deepest condolences. And I'm sorry for what I did. I'll pay for your truck. What I did was stupid. Please forgive me. I told my lawyer to withdraw all charges, so he will be contacting your lawyer soon. Please call me when you can.

Keelan to Elaine: Thank you for your condolences, and thank you for doing that. I will call when I can. I can't call now I hope you understand. But thanks again.

Falling to my knees, I gave God all the glory and all the praise. I let go, and he took charge. "THANK YOU, JESUS!" I shouted at the top of my lungs.

***

Later that day after the interview was over, hundreds of people started to peacefully gather in front of City Hall. Mourners put teddy bears and balloons at the base of the podium in memory of my brother. As the clock struck closer to six, people flooded social media with posts about the event. The streets of downtown Pittsburgh were filled with supporters met by those that we oppose, but we called for a peaceful protest, and my mother asked that after everyone had a chance to speak that everyone disbanded peacefully, in honor of my brother's memory.

The day that Michelle Alexander, the former director of the ACLU Racial Justice Project and Civil Rights Lawyer, called me, many others did too. The day of the "Justice for All March and Speech, many powerful black leaders came to Pittsburgh to support the R.A.I.S.E. U.P. Movement such as Mr. C. West, Al Sharpton, Montague Simmons, Tony Russell, Michael Brown Sr., Lesley McSpadden, Brittany Packnett, and numerous others, including celebrities. Even, my favorite singer, Marsha Ambrosia was there. I got to hold her hand as Pastor Thomas prayed for a peaceful protest. She had started following me on twitter and started retweeting my tweets concerning the R.A.I.S.E U.P. Movement. I sent her a personal message and invited her to the march to my surprise she accepted the invite.

After Michael Eric Dyson had given his speech about the injustices in the black community, police brutality, and all of the powerful black leaders that came before him, our many failures, and the privileges amid our own complaints, he called me to the podium, and the Holy Spirit took over.

"Instead of putting our hands up, we gon' raise up!"

"RAISE UP!" The crowd repeated.

"Instead of putting our hands up, we gon' raise up!"

"RAISE UP!"

"Instead of putting our hands up, we gon' raise up!"

"RAISE UP!"

"Emancipation Proclamation only stands for a black man's incarceration, eradication, refutation and laceration from those with authority. Emancipation Proclamation my ass! FREE...YOU SAY WE'RE FREE...WHAT IS FREEDOM WHEN THOSE AUTHORITY FIGURES STILL HAVE THE POWER TO KILL A FREE MAN! Instead of freedom...We've been free-dumb! Dumb to the facts...Dumb to the solution...Dumb because we don't know what freedom means to us. I say they may give you freedom, but your free-dumb asses bet not smile! They may give you freedom, but I tell your free-dumb asses bet not trust them! Because although they say they gave us freedom, but they withhold THE RIGHT TO VOTE from your free-dumb asses, and although they say they gave us freedom they won't give your free-dumb asses a job. Black incarceration is like black subjugation. There is no equalization! So now my brothers and sisters let us begin self-education. Let's educate ourselves to the fact that we have never been equal in the societies of America. The only equivalent is a black man's freedom papers and a black man's prison release papers. You can come out of slavery or modern day slavery unchained, but your mind is still encaged. Your enraged for a reason but you don't know what that reason is. Let me tell you what those reasons are, YOU CAN'T VOTE, YOU CAN'T GET A JOB, YOU CAN'T GET CREDIT TO OWN LAND, and

YOU'RE CONSTANTLY WATCHING YOUR OWN KIND DIE RAPIDLY! So you're enraged because of lack of purpose and lack of understanding. So thank you, President Lincoln, thank you for nothing! So thank you, President Reagan, thank you for nothing! So thank you, President Obama, thank you for nothing! Because us black boys were in chains and shackles then, and they are in chains and shackles now. Us black boys were dying then, and we're still dying now! And to you police out there, we're black! We're not your punching bags to beat on. We're black! We're not stuff dummies for your canines to chew on. We're black, we not targets to be used for your deadly target practice. Our purpose in this life is not to be left dead in the streets, for a daughter to be fatherless, for a wife to be a widow, a brother to lose a brother, a sister to lose a sister, a father to lose a son, nor a mother to lose her beloved children! Injustice! Injustice! There's no justice! People it's just us! People it's just us! Generations of our people are lost, and we continue to lose as the expansion of America's prison systems are built up to capture and hold to stop us from reproducing, to stop us from voting, to stop us from getting jobs. And Police officer's unholstered weapons are used to fulfill the man's plan to never rehabilitate, but to annihilate and eradicate our race because of the color of our skin! So now we must come together to march like Martin and many other Civil Rights Leaders that have sacrificed their lives just for us to turn Martin's dream into a nightmare. I dare you tell me there's equality. I dare you tell me there's justice! When I continue to see generation after generation of our people die right before our eyes, I dare you tell me to calm down, to be quiet! I dare you to tell me I'm being paranoid, and I'm just overreacting because my mind is full of consciousness, and my eyes see the facts clearly. How does a police officer kill someone's child and get away with it, but if I kill that same child, I go to jail for life? So you tell me where's the equality, you tell me where is the equality!"

"YAAAAAAAY! RAISE UP! RAISE UP! RAISE UP!" I sent the crowd into pandemonium as they shouted.

Leaving the podium, the first one to stop me was Marsha. "That was amazing! I felt that! Hey, I have to leave the country for a few weeks, but when I return I would love for you to join me for a concert I'm doing in New York when I get back," she said as Pastor Thomas tried to calm the crowd down.

"I would love that," I told her.

"Okay, I'll contact you on *Twitter* to get your number. I have to make my flight. Hey, I'm truly sorry about your family, I'll pray for you," she said as she was being pulled away by her assistant telling her that she had to hurry and leave before a riot broke out. That was the only good thing that happened that night. We had called for a peaceful march, but my speech had caused the city to riot for a week straight.

I did interview after interview demanding justice. And we finally got it. Yhey fired the officer that killed my brother and indicted him for murder after one of his co-workers's leaked a racial text message he sent before and after killing my brother. Three days after that the rioting stopped, but my pursuit of a good woman never did. Teal had tried to call, but I didn't accept her call, and I didn't reply to any of her messages. The same happened with Clarissa and Mereza. Payton and

I was finally on speaking terms. She had really stood up for my family on her show, making me have a new found love for her. I wasn't in love with her, but I loved her.

Chapter 20

THAT WHICH IS BEFORE YOU

A month after my brother's death, I was packing the last of my things to go to New York to see Marsha in concert. Since the Justice For All Speech, we had kept in contact with each other, Skype'd. texted or talked on the phone. I couldn't believe that my life journey had put me on the path with a woman that I had fallen in love with through music. I truly believed that our fling could turn into something serious.

"Wy', you want me to bring you back anything from New York," I called and asked Wyoni. She was home now and doing well. She still couldn't walk, and her speech was still slurred a little.

"I don't know, just bring me something," she said with a slur.

"Aight, I got you," I told her.

"What time does you plane leave?" She asked.

"At one," I told her. It was eleven o'clock, but I wanted to leave early.

"Oh, okay. How long are you going to be gone?" She asked.

"I'm not sure. She asked if I had my passport, so ain't no telling. We might end up anywhere. The way she talking, we might make this thing official, Wy'. God may have sent me the good woman I've been so desperately looking for." There was a silence on the phone when I said that. "Wy'?!" I called out.

"Yea, I'm here."

"You okay, your nurse is there ain't she?"

"Yea, she's here," she said.

"Aight look, I'll call when I get to New York, aight? Love you."

"Alright. Love you, too."

On the way to the airport, I listened to *Daley* featuring my new baby, *Marsha Ambrosia* sing:

Ya almost exactly what I need-eed
a definite maybe...I can't help to think that
this don't add up
I'm try'na separate all the fact
from fiction
And if, baby, ya the truth

then I'm lying next to you...

KEELAN TO MARSHA: On my way to N-Y, baby.

MARSHA TO KEELAN: Can't wait to see you, my love.

Once I arrived at Greater International Airport, I parked my car and rolled my luggage to the Check-In line. Standing in line, I thought about all of the crazy experiences I had with all of the women in my life. From the fight at the church to going to jail to having sex all the time to not having sex to having multiple women to not having a woman in my life, my search for a good woman has been a crazy rollercoaster ride. And here I was, I was traveling to New York to be with a beautiful woman that I would have never thought in my wildest dreams that I would be with, but it was happening. God was coming through for me again. He was sending me ah good woman.

Other than that, *Barber Cheers* was being picked up by Tidal, my mother was looking at a multi-million dollar lawsuit against the City of Pittsburgh, and Wyoni was getting better. I missed my brother, but I felt that I had did him justice by getting justice. The R.A.I.S.E U.P. Movement was alive and vibrant, and all this was because I remained faithful to my God. Also standing there, I thought about my ex-wife, Payton, and I reached into my shoulder bag and pulled out the letter she had written me. I still had not read it. Tearing it open, I didn't know what to expect.

"Dear Keelan..."

"Keelan! KEELAN!"

I started reading Payton's letter then I heard a familiar voice calling out my name with a slur. It was Wyoni. Her nurse was wheeling her wheelchair towards the Check-In line.

"What are you doing here Wy'?" I asked puzzled by her being at the airport.

"Keelan, don't go. I love you. I've always loved," she admitted.

I stepped out of line and stood in silence as my heart started to pick up its pace. Wyoni had everyone's attention including mine.

"I'm ya good woman, Keelan. All of these years I've been waiting for you to realize that. God been put me...Aaah..." Wyoni stood out of her wheelchair.

"Wy'?!" I said starting to walk to her, but she stopped me.

"No, Keelan, I'll come to you. That's how much strength your love gives me. It drives me to do the impossible..." she said, taking a step. Her nurse caught her as she almost fell. The onlookers gasped. I took a step towards her and stopped. Then she took another step on her own. That's when I noticed a small ring box in her hand. "Like I was saying, God been put me in your life. God put you in my life. You're my good man, and I'm your good woman. Keelan, will you..." She was face to face with me. "Will you marry me?"

"AAAWWW...OH MY GOD...HE BETTER SAY, YES!" The onlookers commented.

"Yes Wy', yes, I will marry you!" I answered with the biggest grin on my face.

Made in the USA
Columbia, SC
02 October 2024